The Easter Rising

☙ A GUIDE TO DUBLIN IN 1916 ☙

Conor Kostick and Lorcan Collins

To Aoife and Conor – future rebels

Lorcan Collins merged his interest in Irish history and Dublin's culture by founding the 1916 Rebellion Walking Tour. He regularly contributes to topical magazines and is currently writing full time. Lorcan studied history and literature in UCD.

Conor Kostick is an historian and writer. He has written for several journals and newspapers on history, politics and contemporary art. He is currently continuing his history studies at Trinity College, Dublin, with a focus on medieval history.

The 1916 Rebellion Walking Tour has been in operation since 1996. The tour gives participants an understanding of the complex events of twentieth-century Ireland. Visiting the sites of the Easter Rising, the War of Independence and the Civil War provides an excellent platform for explanation, discussion and debate. The tours have proven to be very popular and are guided by Lorcan Collins and Conor Kostick. Information is available from www.1916rising.com

The EASTER RISING

A Guide To Dublin In 1916

Conor Kostick • Lorcan Collins

THE O'BRIEN PRESS
DUBLIN

First published 2000 by The O'Brien Press Ltd.,
20 Victoria Road, Dublin 6, Ireland.
Tel: +353 1 4923333; Fax: +353 1 4922777
E-mail: books@obrien.ie
Website: www.obrien.ie
Reprinted 2001.

ISBN: 0-86278-638-X

British Library Cataloguing-in-Publication Data
Kostick, Conor, 1964-
The Easter Rising : a guide to Dublin in 1916
1.Ireland - History - Easter Rising, 1916 2.Dublin (Ireland) -
Guidebooks
I.Title II.Collins, Lorcan
941-5'0821

2 3 4 5 6 7 8 9 10
01 02 03 04 05 06 07

The O'Brien Press receives
assistance from

The Arts Council
An Chomhairle Ealaíon

Editing, layout and design: The O'Brien Press Ltd.
Map (pp.12–13): Design Image
Colour separations: C&A Print Services Ltd.
Printing: Leinster Leader

CONTENTS

ACKNOWLEDGEMENTS

The authors would like to thank the following: John, James, Alan, Simon, John, Peter and the rest of the lads at the International Bar, Wicklow Street; the staff at the military archives, Cathal Brugha barracks; Helen Litton; our comrades at The O'Brien Press; Jane Fitzpatrick and all at Dublin Tourism; John deCourcy Ireland; Gavin Kostick; John Brown, James Harte and Gráinne MacLouchlainn and Eoin O'Driscoll at the National Photographic Archive; all in the GPO; Niamh O'Sullivan at Kilmainham Gaol and Museum; Pat Cooke at the Pearse Museum; Colin Smythe; Aoife O'Shea at the National Museum; Treasa Collins; and for personal encouragement Trish Darcy, Diarmuid, Dermo, Orla and Mark, Earl Gerry, Barbara Whiston, Larry Shaw, Elaine Moore, David Turner and finally 'Booster'. The quotes from W.B. Yeats appear by permission of A.P. Watt Ltd on behalf of Michael B. Yeats, courtesy of the publishers. The quotes from Seán O'Casey appear courtesy of Faber and Faber. The excerpt from Thomas Kinsella's translation of the *Táin* is reproduced with permission from the author. The poems by Patrick Kavanagh are reproduced by kind permission of the Trustees of the Estate of Katherine Kavanagh.

Picture credits

The authors and publisher thank the following for permission to use photographs & illustrative material: Dúchas, the Heritage Service for p.32; National Museum/Collins Barracks for pp.53, 69, 78, 99, 102, 127 (both), 128, 129; John deCourcey Ireland for p.33; Kilmainham Gaol and Museum for pp.20, 77, 96, 121; RTÉ for pp.16–17, 41, 64, 86, 87, 103, 107, 131, 138; Courtesy of the National Library of Ireland pp.21 (KE 44, Arthur Griffith at his desk), 23 (KE 53, Seán Mac Diarmada), 24 (KE 235, Tom Clarke), 25 (KE 77, Eoin MacNeill), 28 (KE 198, Citizen Army on parade outside Liberty Hall), 31 (KE 9, Roger Casement), 42 (KE 47, Eamonn Ceannt), 51 (KE 212, Fianna Éireann Council in 1915 with Con Colbert), 52 (KE 46, Seán Heuston in uniform), 54 (KE 20, Collins), 59 (Alb 196, Butt Bridge and dome of Custom House), 61 (Alb 196, House on Clanwilliam Place), 66 (KE 26, de Valera in uniform), 75 (KE 81, The Countess), 90 (Alb 196, 1. GPO with boy pulling cart), 91 (Alb 196, 19. Side view of GPO portico), 92 (Alb 196, 25. Interior of GPO with man on ladder), 104 (KE 98, William Pearse), 106 (Alb 196, 15. Four Courts with bullet holes), 111 (KE 55, Thomas MacDonagh), 119 (KE 23, Ned Daly in uniform); Colin Smythe Publishing Ltd for pp.29, 44 (both), 47 (both), 84, 85, 94, 97, 108, 118 (both), 120, 122, 123 (both). Thanks to Paula Geraghty for photographs on pp.1, 71; Pictures on pp.1, 14, 49, 71, 72 are the authors' own.

The drawings of the military positions held during the Rising are the original work of the late Colonel P.J. Hally and appeared in the *Irish Sword*, Volume 7. We are very pleased to thank the Irish Military History Society for permission to reproduce information based on the original work. Map designed by Design Image.

The publisher and authors have made every reasonable effort to contact the copyright holders of material reproduced in this book. If any involuntary infringement of copyright has occurred, sincere apologies are offered and the owners of such copyright are requested to contact the publisher.

Preface

There is always the danger that when history is written and subsequently read, the events described assume an unreal, almost fictional form. One of the great pleasures in walking among historic streets and buildings is that the vividness and actuality of history returns. All the more so when bullet holes provide scars which serve as a stark reminder of conflict. Men and women who really existed, who, like us, held powerful ideas and emotions, stood in these very places, hearts racing.

This book is drawn from the popular 1916 Rebellion Walking Tour. The events of Easter 1916 are described, not in order of when they took place, but through the incidents that would have taken place at the various points along the tour. Each chapter is based on the immediate surroundings of the stop in question. To include significant incidents from further afield, descriptions of events that occurred away from the city centre have been included towards the end of the chapters, with appropriate map references.

If you are unable to visit Dublin or follow the route of the tour, then it is simplicity itself to mentally follow the route of the map. If you were to walk from stop to stop, as we recommend, it would take about an hour and a half. In either case there are plenty of photographs to help your imagination recreate a sense of what was an extraordinarily dramatic time.

Timeline of Events leading up to the Easter Rising

1 November 1884 The Gaelic Athletic Association (GAA) founded to promote Irish sport and games. The association denies membership to the police and army and is immediately infiltrated by the Irish Republican Brotherhood (IRB).

8 April 1886 First Home Rule Bill for Ireland presented by William Gladstone, the Liberal Prime Minister of Britain, to the House of Commons.

8 June 1886 First Home Rule Bill defeated by 343 votes to 313.

31 July 1893 Gaelic League founded by Douglas Hyde and Eoin MacNeill in order to encourage Irish people to speak the language and take a greater interest in their culture.

1 September 1893 Gladstone's Second Home Rule Bill passed by House of Commons but vetoed by the House of Lords by 419 votes to 41.

September 1900 Cumann na nGaedheal (Irish Council) founded by Arthur Griffith in order to promote a 'buy Irish' campaign.

1903 National Council formed by Griffith to protest the proposed visit of Edward VII to Ireland. The Council attracts members such as W.B. Yeats and Maud Gonne.

1905 Dungannon Clubs founded in Ulster to promote separatism from Britain. Bulmer Hobson and Denis McCullogh, IRB revivalists, were the main organisers of these societies.

1905–08 Cumann na nGaedheal, the National Council and the Dungannon Clubs are amalgamated to form Sinn Féin (Ourselves Alone).

December 1908 The foundation of James Larkin's radical Irish Transport and General Workers' Union (ITGWU).

August 1909 Countess Markievicz and Bulmer Hobson organise nationalist youths into Na Fianna Éireann (Warriors of Ireland) a kind of rebel Boy Scout brigade. Many members were later to join the IRB.

April 1912 Herbert Asquith introduces the Third Home Rule Bill to the British Parliament. Passed by the Commons and rejected by the Lords, the Bill would have to become law due to the Parliament Act. Home Rule expected to be introduced for Ireland by autumn 1914.

January 1913 Sir Edward Carson and James Craig set up Ulster Volunteer Force (UVF) with the intention of defending Ulster against Home Rule.

1913–14 Dublin Lockout: William Martin Murphy leads the employers in a bitter dispute against the ITGWU.

31 August 1913 Massive ITGWU protest rally on Sackville Street [now O'Connell Street] attacked by the Dublin Metropolitan Police. Two strikers killed by the police.

23 November 1913 James Larkin and James Connolly establish the Irish Citizen Army in order to protect strikers.

25 November 1913 The Irish Volunteers founded in Dublin to 'secure the rights and liberties common to all the people of Ireland'. By 1914 their ranks swell to 100,000. In line with the Volunteers, a women's league, (Cumann na mBan) is founded and organised by Countess Markievicz, Agnes O'Farrelly and Mary MacSwiney.

24 April 1914 A shipment of 25,000 rifles and 3 million rounds of ammunition are landed at Larne, County Antrim, for the UVF.

26 July 1914 Irish Volunteers unload a shipment of 1,500 rifles and 45,000 rounds of ammunition freshly arrived from Germany aboard Erskine Childers' yacht the *Asgard*. British troops fire on jeering crowd on Bachelors Walk, Dublin, killing three citizens.

4 August 1914 First World War declared. Home Rule for Ireland shelved for the duration of the war with Germany.

9 September 1914 Meeting held at Gaelic League headquarters between IRB and other extreme republicans. Initial decision made to stage an uprising while Britain is at war.

20 September 1914 John Redmond urges Irish Volunteers to enlist in the British Army. A split occurs in the movement as 170,000 leave the Volunteers and form the National Volunteers or Redmondites. Only 11,000 remain as the Irish Volunteers under Eoin MacNeill.

May–September 1915 Military Council of the IRB is formed consisting of Pádraic Pearse, Joseph Mary Plunkett, Eamonn Ceannt, Seán Mac Diarmada and Thomas Clarke. These men take effective control of the plans for the Rising.

August 1915 Pearse gives fiery oration at the funeral of Jeremiah O'Donovan Rossa warning Britain that 'Ireland unfree shall never be at peace'.

November–December 1915 Military Council manipulation ensures Denis McCullough becomes president of the IRB. McCullough has no knowledge of the Military Council or their plans.

19 January 1916 James Connolly encouraged to join the IRB and is voted onto the Military Council thus ensuring that the Irish Citizen Army shall be involved in the Rising. Thomas MacDonagh becomes the seventh member of the Military Council several weeks later. Rising date confirmed for Easter Sunday.

9 April 1916 The *Libau* sets sail from Lubeck in Germany. Captain Karl Spindler changes the name of the vessel to the *Aud* to avoid detection by the British, who would be very interested in her cargo of 20,000 rifles, ten machine-guns and a million rounds of ammunition, bound for Tralee Bay on the southwest coast of Ireland.

12 April 1916 Sir Roger Casement boards submarine U-19 at Wilmshaven, Germany, bound for a rendezvous with the *Aud* at

Tralee. With him are Robert Monteith, an IRB man, and Sergeant Daniel Bailey, a former prisoner of war who had joined Casement's Irish Brigade. Casement is tired and ill after many months in Germany seeking military assistance for the Rising.

19 April 1916 Alderman Kelly reads the Castle Order to a meeting of Dublin Corporation. This forged document, supposedly from Dublin Castle, indicated that there was to be mass arrests of Irish Volunteers to prevent 'trouble'.

20 April, 4.15pm The *Aud* arrives at Tralee Bay. As the local Volunteers expect the ship to arrive on Easter Saturday, the arms are not landed. Spindler waits in vain for a signal from shore.

21 April, 2.15am Roger Casement and his two companions go ashore from U-19 and land on Banna Strand. Bailey and Monteith go to seek the local Volunteers. Hours later Casement is discovered at McKenna's Fort and is arrested by the Royal Irish Constabulary.

6.30pm The *Aud* is captured by the British Navy and forced to sail towards Cork Harbour.

22 April, 1am Karl Spindler and his crew scuttle the *Aud* to prevent her precious cargo falling into enemy hands. The weapons for the Rising are lost to the sea off Daunt's Rock.

10pm Eoin MacNeill, as Chief of Staff of the Irish Volunteers, issues the countermanding order in Dublin to try to stop the Rising. Michael Joseph O'Rahilly (known as 'The O'Rahilly') embarks on a journey to the south with these orders.

23 April, 9am The Military Council meet to discuss the situation considering MacNeill has placed an advertisement in a Sunday newspaper halting all Volunteer operations. The Rising is put on hold for twenty-four hours. Hundreds of copies of *The Proclamation of the Republic* are printed in Liberty Hall.

24 April, 12 noon The 1916 Rising begins in Dublin.

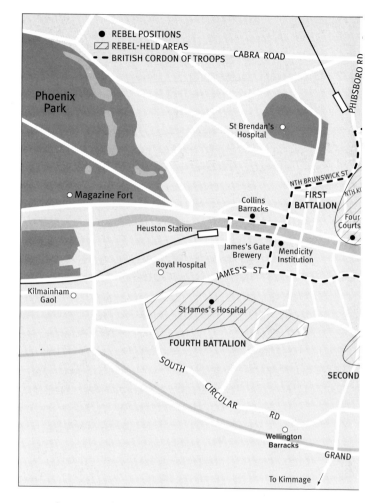

Modern names of streets and places are used on the map.
The following guide indicates their former names.

MODERN NAME	NAME IN 1916
Beggars Bush Building	Beggars Bush Barracks
Broadstone	Broadstone Railway Terminus
Cathal Brugha Barracks	Portobello Barracks
Collins Barracks	Royal Barracks
Connolly Station	Amiens Street Railway Station
Dún Laoghaire Harbour	Kingstown Harbour

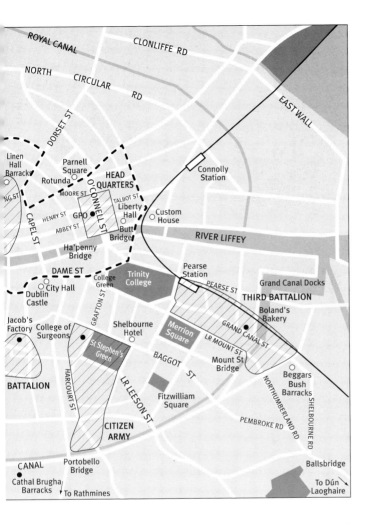

MODERN NAME	NAME IN 1916
Griffith Barracks	Wellington Barracks
Heuston Station	Kingsbridge Railway Station
O'Connell Street	Sackville Street
Pearse Station	Westland Row Railway Station
St Brendan's Hospital	North Dublin Union
St James's Hospital	South Dublin Union

POBLACHT NA H EIREANN.

THE PROVISIONAL GOVERNMENT
OF THE

IRISH REPUBLIC
TO THE PEOPLE OF IRELAND.

IRISHMEN AND IRISHWOMEN : In the name of God and of the dead generations from which she receives her old tradition of nationhood, Ireland, through us, summons her children to her flag and strikes for her freedom.

Having organised and trained her manhood through her secret revolutionary organisation, the Irish Republican Brotherhood, and through her open military organisations, the Irish Volunteers and the Irish Citizen Army, having patiently perfected her discipline, having resolutely waited for the right moment to reveal itself, she now seizes that moment, and, supported by her exiled children in America and by gallant allies in Europe, but relying in the first on her own strength, she strikes in full confidence of victory.

We declare the right of the people of Ireland to the ownership of Ireland, and to the unfettered control of Irish destinies, to be sovereign and indefeasible. The long usurpation of that right by a foreign people and government has not extinguished the right, nor can it ever be extinguished except by the destruction of the Irish people. In every generation the Irish people have asserted their right to national freedom and sovereignty : six times during the past three hundred years they have asserted it in arms. Standing on that fundamental right and again asserting it in arms in the face of the world, we hereby proclaim the Irish Republic as a Sovereign Independent State, and we pledge our lives and the lives of our comrades-in-arms to the cause of its freedom, of its welfare; and of its exaltation among the nations.

The Irish Republic is entitled to, and hereby claims, the allegiance of every Irishman and Irishwoman. The Republic guarantees religious and civil liberty, equal rights and equal opportunities to all its citizens, and declares its resolve to pursue the happiness and prosperity of the whole nation and of all its parts, cherishing all the children of the nation equally, and oblivious of the differences carefully fostered by an alien government, which have divided a minority from the majority in the past.

Until our arms have brought the opportune moment for the establishment of a permanent National Government, representative of the whole people of Ireland and elected by the suffrages of all her men and women, the Provisional Government, hereby constituted, will administer the civil and military affairs of the Republic in trust for the people.

We place the cause of the Irish Republic under the protection of the Most High God, Whose blessing we invoke upon our arms, and we pray that no one who serves that cause will dishonour it by cowardice, inhumanity, or rapine. In this supreme hour the Irish nation must, by its valour and discipline and by the readiness of its children to sacrifice themselves for the common good, prove itself worthy of the august destiny to which it is called.

Signed on Behalf of the Provisional Government,

THOMAS J. CLARKE,
SEAN Mac DIARMADA,   THOMAS MacDONAGH,
P. H. PEARSE,   EAMONN CEANNT,
JAMES CONNOLLY.   JOSEPH PLUNKETT

The Proclamation of the Republic of Ireland (Poblacht na hÉireann)
was printed in Liberty Hall on Sunday, the day before the Easter Rising.
Liam Ó Briain, Christopher Brady and Michael Molloy printed approximately
2,500 copies on the *Workers' Republic* printing press.

INTRODUCTION

DUBLIN IN 1916

Dublin in 1916 was a city of extraordinary contradictions. Still growing, with its population at around 400,000, it had also witnessed a marked decline from its glory days of the eighteenth century – when it had been amongst the pre-eminent cities of Europe. A century of uneven and wavering development had followed the Act of Union of 1801, an Act which linked Ireland and England more closely, and abolished the Irish Parliament. Economic decay, encompassing the Great Famine of 1845–1848, had led to the growth of the darker side of the city. Slum tenements had encroached upon the huge weighty public buildings of the eighteenth century, so that they no longer appeared as spacious monuments to prosperity, but rather as 'big stones' among the rubble.

Twenty-five thousand families lived in tenements, seventy-eight percent in single-room dwellings; the two Dublin workhouses contained 6,500 paupers. The previous year pawnbrokers had taken four and a half million pledges. Accompanying the overcrowding and poverty were the deadly diseases of tuberculosis and pneumonia – which contributed to the grim statistic that while infant mortality was 103 per 1,000 live births in London in 1914, it was 142 for Dublin.

Next page: Sackville Street [now O'Connell Street]. After the Rising the centre of Dublin was thronged with visitors wishing to view the destruction and perhaps gain a better understanding of the events surrounding Easter Week.

Yet the Great War was bringing in new wealth for some. In 1916, Ireland's linen, bacon, cattle, poultry, wool and sheep exports were double those of 1904. The trams were bustling, the port busy with shipping. Prosperity, alongside poverty, was reflected in an informal division of the two sides of Sackville Street [now O'Connell Street]: one for the respectable classes to walk along; the other the terrain of the 'shawlies', Dublin's female poor, wearing their characteristic garment and quick to pass sharp observations on any unfortunate who might stray into their territory from the other side of the street.

While the gap between rich and poor in the city in 1916 was wider than ever, the last generation had witnessed one distinctive and important demographic change. A new Catholic middle class had developed and their houses formed the sprawling suburbs of the south side of the city. Their savings filled the deposits of the banks (which had doubled from 1890 to 1910) and their interests stimulated a revival in matters Irish: namely the history, the culture, the language and the sports.

This class formed the backbone of a renewed pride in Irish identity, and the Gaelic revival represented the overcoming of the post-famine years of demoralisation. The **Gaelic Athletic Association**, founded in 1884 to promote Gaelic sports, was thriving, as was the **Gaelic League**, founded in 1893, whose promotion of Irish language and culture gained it a mass following. By 1906 it had 900 branches with 100,000 members.

Dublin was vibrant with social and cultural events, celebrating a somewhat mythical Irish past. This was the milieu in which political radicals strove to win supporters, an appropriate backdrop for the range of political voices and outlooks that existed within the city.

Dublin Castle Administration

Since the Act of Union had taken effect, Irish political affairs were controlled and directed from the Westminster Parliament in London. Leading the Irish administration was the Lord Lieutenant of Ireland, who lived in the Viceregal Lodge, Phoenix Park. In 1916 Lord Wimborne had recently been appointed to this position. His authority was largely symbolic and the civil service, based in Dublin Castle, ran the country in practical terms. At the head of the civil service stood the Chief Secretary for Ireland, who in 1916 was Augustine Birrell. Birrell was a close associate of the British Prime Minister, Herbert Asquith, and since the outbreak of the First World War had been spending the bulk of his time in London. This meant that responsibility for the day-to-day governing of Ireland fell on the permanent under-secretary, **Sir Matthew Nathan**.

Nathan was in a peculiar position in 1916. Ireland had been promised **Home Rule**, that is, a large measure of self-government such as that obtained by Canada or Australia. An alliance of Liberal Party and Irish MPs had faced down a revolt from the House of Lords, and brought a Home Rule Bill for Ireland forward in 1914. Nathan should have been put in a position of having to prepare the administration for a take-over by a new Irish government, and to that end he kept in touch with the potential future leaders of such a government, John Redmond and John Dillon, leaders of the **Irish Parliamentary Party**. However, very determined opposition from the British Conservative Party and Irish Unionists had seriously undermined the prospect of Home Rule for Ireland.

One part of Ireland to prosper from the connection with the British Empire had been the northeastern area, around Belfast. Determined to maintain their economic success, which they saw as being dependent on their link to Britain, Northern industrialists founded the **Ulster Unionist Council** in 1885. Although claiming to represent all Protestants in Ireland, the organisation was not so much concerned with religion as economics. For them prosperity and the Protestant work ethic were bound up with remaining British. In their view, papal rule and ruin were threatened with the introduction of Home Rule for Ireland.

When lobbying looked likely to be insufficient, the Unionists turned to force, and defied the government by creating a paramilitary organisation in 1912, the **Ulster Volunteer Force**. This private army became a serious force in Irish politics following the illegal landing of 25,000 rifles and three million rounds of ammunition at Larne on 24 April 1914. A month earlier, British officers at the Curragh Camp, in County Kildare, had threatened to resign rather than clamp down on the UVF. Instead of confronting this combination of mutinous and illegal activity, the British government backed away from the goal of Home Rule for Ireland. The idea of partitioning Ireland gathered strength, and the whole issue was postponed with the entry of Britain into the Great War that

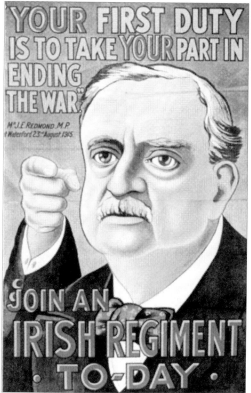

Based on the famous Kitchener recruiting poster, this caricature of John Redmond was used to encourage Irish Volunteers to enlist in the British Army during the First World War.

August.

So for Matthew Nathan, the main concern was to continue the administration of Ireland during the war, while monitoring the activities of radicals who might challenge British rule, and assisting the military in their efforts to raise Irish recruits for the British Army overseas.

Nathan knew he could depend on one group, the Catholic middle classes, and their political representatives, the Irish Parliamentary Party. Led by John Redmond, this party voiced the concerns of respectable Catholic business and landowners and had close allies in the hierarchy of the Irish Catholic Church.

NATIONALIST POLITICS

On 3 August 1914, Redmond put the support of his party behind the British war effort. He hoped that if Ireland proved its loyalty during the crisis, the passage of Home Rule would be more likely to be implemented following the war. Redmond actively encouraged Irishmen to fight on behalf of Britain. Radical Irish nationalism, however, absolutely opposed this approach, believing rather in the old Fenian slogan that 'England's difficulty is Ireland's opportunity'. This radicalism manifested itself in a number of organisations in Dublin in 1916.

Sinn Féin

Sinn Féin (Ourselves Alone) was a political party, founded in 1905 and led by Arthur Griffith, publisher of the newspaper of the same name. Although the Easter Rising subsequently became associated with Sinn Féin, Griffith's party was not involved in

Arthur Griffith, journalist, economist, intellectual and founder of Sinn Féin.

any military activity. Rather it set out a political programme of independence for Ireland, not necessarily a republic nor involving a complete break from the Empire. Griffith raised the example of the joint Austria-Hungary monarchy as a possible model for British-Irish relations. Where Sinn Féin were more radical than the Irish Parliamentary Party, and thus gained support, was in their conviction that elected Irish representatives should not take up their seats in Westminster but should remain in Ireland to create an Irish government.

Irish Republican Brotherhood

The **Irish Republican Brotherhood** (IRB) were the main instigators of the Easter Rising. A secret society, they were descendants of the Fenian movement of the 1850s. Fenianism advocated separation by physical force and had once had some 40,000 to 50,000 members. However, its popularity had been checked by military repression after a failed rising, and its only lasting organisational legacy was the IRB and its sister group, **Clan na nGael** (The Irish Family) in America. Despite its meagre 2,000 membership in 1912, and its dependency on subsidies from Clan na nGael, the IRB was emerging from a long period of passivity and decline. A new spirit had taken hold of the organisation, represented by the appearance of a newspaper, *Irish Freedom*, edited by Bulmer Hobson. Hobson had played an important role for the IRB in his home province of Ulster, with his organisation of the 'Dungannon Clubs', societies for promoting Irish independence.

An important recruit to the Dungannon Clubs was Seán Mac Diarmada, whose energy and speaking skills were quickly spotted by the IRB. From 1907 to 1911, Mac Diarmada toured Ireland re-

SEÁN MAC DIARMADA

Originally from County Leitrim, Seán Mac Diarmada worked as a gardener in Glasgow and later as a tram conductor. While in Belfast Mac Diarmada was recruited to the IRB and was sent to Dublin in 1908 to revitalise the organisation. Popular as a speaker,

Mac Diarmada journeyed throughout the west, often by bicycle, reorganising the IRB – to whose Supreme Council he was appointed, as Treasurer. Following the outbreak of war, Mac Diarmada was sentenced to three months in prison for a fiery anti-recruitment speech – provoked by the 'slavish pro-British' attitude of his audience in County Galway.

organising the movement.

Not all of the older IRB members responded enthusiastically to the changes, but one Fenian veteran, Tom Clarke, welcomed the more outward-looking approach. Clarke and Mac Diarmada struck up a deep friendship.

They believed that England would never concede Irish independence unless she was forced to do so, and they could see the likelihood of Home Rule arriving via parliamentary means fading away. Their real opportunity for action emerged with the establishment of a nationalist equivalent to the UVF, the **Irish Volunteers,** through which the revived IRB was able to recruit new and talented members, such as Pádraic Pearse [*see* Chapter 2], Thomas MacDonagh, Joseph Plunkett and Eamonn Ceannt, from the general milieu of cultural Irish nationalism.

Seán Mac Diarmada was an IRB revivalist, a founding member of the Irish Volunteers, Secretary of the Supreme Council of the IRB, a member of the IRB Military Council and a signatory of the Proclamation. He was one of the guiding forces behind the Rising. Mac Diarmada fought in the GPO and was executed in Kilmainham Gaol on 12 May 1916.

Thomas J. Clarke was a Fenian, an explosives expert, a shopkeeper, a quiet gentleman but also a dedicated IRB revivalist and member of the IRB Military Council. He spent many years in British prisons. The first to sign the Proclamation, Clarke was in the GPO during the Rising and was executed in Kilmainham Gaol on 3 May 1916.

TOM CLARKE

Tom Clarke was the key figure who linked the previous generation of revolutionary nationalists – the Fenians – with the new IRB activists. Clarke had returned to Dublin in 1907 from a lifelong involvement in the Fenian conspiracies in England, Ireland and America (one consequence of which had been a sentence of fifteen years imprisonment in England). Clarke's newspaper and tobacco shop in Great Britain Street [now Parnell Street] became a notorious centre for nationalist activity. The Secretary of the Post Office in Ireland, giving evidence of precautions against disloyalty, declared that:

> It seemed safe to classify as dangerous those who were credibly reported to be in more than occasional or chance communication with some one or some of the small group of persons known in Dublin to be dangerously seditious, eg. T.J. Clarke.

THOMAS MacDONAGH

A poet and a playwright, MacDonagh followed his friend and colleague Pádraic Pearse into the IRB. MacDonagh was a tutor of English Literature in University College, Dublin, and had helped Pearse set up St Enda's School in Rathfarnham. Like Joseph Plunkett, MacDonagh directed the Irish Theatre in Hardwicke Street. His play *When the Dawn is Come* was produced at the Abbey Theatre in 1908.

EAMONN CEANNT

A founder member of the Gaelic League, Ceannt was one of the younger generation of radicals recruited to the IRB. He stood in some sympathy with Connolly's socialist views, defending workers' rights in the pages of *Sinn Féin*. At the time of the Rising, Ceannt held an important clerical position in the Treasurer's office.

Irish Volunteers

In November 1913 the Gaelic League paper, *An Claidheamh Soluis* (The Sword of Light), carried an article arguing that the Unionists had shown the way forward and that nationalists should now organise an armed force of volunteers, despite the presence of the British Army. This article had considerable impact as it was the initiative of Eoin Mac-Neill, Professor of early Irish history at University College, Dublin. Mac-Neill was not perceived as an extremist, rather as a respectable scholar and political moderate.

Eoin MacNeill was a Professor of Irish History, a Gaelic League organiser, the Irish Volunteers Chief of Staff. He issued the countermanding order resulting in mass confusion before the Rising. MacNeill resigned from the Volunteers the night before the Rising and became a TD for the Free State Government in later years.

IRB members approached Mac-Neill, without revealing the IRB's existence to him, and at a successful meeting the new Irish Volunteers were launched, with 3,000 to 4,000 members. By May 1914, 75,000 had enrolled. Redmond pushed his followers into taking over the Volunteers in June 1914, a move reluctantly accepted by MacNeill in the interests of nationalist unity. With the outbreak of the First World War, this unity was shattered as Redmond promised the Volunteers to the British Army. The IRB and MacNeill opposed this move. While some 170,000 volunteers followed Redmond, only about 11,000 remained in the Irish Volunteers of the radicals.

Within the Irish Volunteers there remained important political differences. The IRB members generally believed that an insurrection had to be attempted while England was at war and at its weakest, to galvanise the population, while leaders of the Volunteers such as MacNeill and Bulmer Hobson thought a Rising should only be attempted if it were forced upon them by a British crackdown or by the imposition of conscription. This divergence was to result in disastrous confusion in 1916.

Irish Citizen Army

One further strand to radical nationalism was an organisation unique to Dublin, the **Irish Citizen Army** (ICA). This was a further body of volunteers, equipped and drilled in defiance of the administration and consisting of socialist workers. It dated back to the Dublin Lockout of 1913. This Lockout, fought on the issue of the recognition of James Larkin's radical union, the Irish Transport and General Workers' Union, began when William Martin Murphy, a prominent industrialist, locked out a number of trade unionists on 19 August 1913. The conflict escalated until it involved 400 employers and 25,000 workers. Almost all of Dublin came to an economic standstill, but after six months, hungry and embittered, the workforce returned defeated.

At a mass meeting, following police attacks on assemblies of workers during the dispute, Jim Larkin had called for volunteers to form a Citizen Army to defend meetings and marches:

> If Sir Edward can call on the people of Ulster to arm, I will call upon you to arm. If they have a right to arm, the working men have an equal right to arm so as to protect themselves.

REASONS WHY

YOU SHOULD JOIN

The Irish Citizen Army.

BECAUSE It pledges its members to work for, organise for, drill for and fight for **an Independent Ireland.**

BECAUSE It places its reliance upon the only class that never betrayed Ireland—the Irish Working Class.

BECAUSE Having a definite aim to work for there is no fear of it being paralysed in the moment of action by divisions in its Executive Body.

BECAUSE It teaches that "the sole right of ownership of Ireland is vested in the people of Ireland, and that that full right of ownership may, and ought to be, enforced by any and all means that God hath put within the power of man."

BECAUSE It works in harmony with the Labour and true National Movements and thus embraces all that makes for Social Welfare and National Dignity.

Companies Wanted in Every District.

RECRUITS WANTED EVERY HOUR.

Apply for further information, Secretary, Citizen Army, Liberty Hall, Dublin.

Irish Paper.]   *City Printing Works, 13 Stafford Street, Dublin.*

Irish Citizen Army recruiting poster.

SIR EDWARD CARSON

Born in Dublin in 1854, Edward Carson was drawn from a solid Loyalist background. He studied law at Trinity College and as a young man became assistant to the Chief Secretary of Ireland, Arthur Balfour, who made him Ireland's Solicitor-General in 1892. A Member of Parliament for Dublin University, Carson became notorious as the prosecutor in the Oscar Wilde trial. From 1911 Carson began to work closely with Ulster Unionists, becoming one of their most effective speakers and political organisers against Home Rule in Ireland.

The Citizen Army suffered from the defeat of the strike, but survived. Drilled by Captain Jack White, its members undertook both

Irish Citizen Army parade outside Liberty Hall.

military training and political instruction from James Connolly [*see* Chapter 4]. In the basement of Liberty Hall, office of the ITGWU, arms were packed and bombs were made.

As the Citizen Army was the only military force that accepted women members – the Irish Volunteers had formed a women's non-combatant auxiliary, **Cumann na mBan** (Women's League) – it attracted a number of women fighters, most prominently Count-

Liberty Hall, headquarters of the Irish Transport and General Workers' Union (ITGWU) and the Irish Citizen Army, pictured following bombardment by shellfire from the *Helga* gunboat.

ess Markievicz, the Honorary Treasurer and one of the better shots in the army. Born into an aristocratic Anglo-Irish family, she had been converted to militant socialism by James Connolly.

Throughout 1914 and 1915 the Citizen Army remained small, with just over 200 members, but it achieved a high degree of military competence under Chief of Staff Michael Mallin, winning the first prize in drill and arms handling at a competition for volun-

Oglaigh na hEireann.

ENROL UNDER THE GREEN FLAG.

Safeguard your rights and liberties (the few left you).

Secure more.

Help your Country to a place among the nations.

Give her a National Army to keep her there.

Get a gun and do your part.

JOIN THE

IRISH VOLUNTEERS

(President: EOIN MAC NEILL).

The local Company drills at _____

_____

Ireland shall no longer remain disarmed and impotent.

A 1914 Irish Volunteers' recruitment poster.

EQUIPMENT.   **Leaflet A 1,**

fianna fáil.
THE IRISH VOLUNTEERS

SERVICE KIT.

The following are the articles prescribed by Headquarters for the personal equipment of Volunteers on field service. Items printed in **heavy type** are to be regarded as important:

FOR ALL VOLUNTEERS.

(a.) As to clothes: uniform or other clothes as preferred; if uniform not worn clothes to be of neutral colour; nothing white or shiny (white collar not to be worn); **soft-brimmed hat** (to be worn in lieu of cap on field service); strong comfortable boots; overcoat.

(b.) As to arms: **rifle,** with sling and **cleaning outfit;** 100 rounds of **ammunition,** with bandolier or ammunition pouches to hold same; **bayonet,** with scabbard, frog and belt; strong knife or slasher.

(c.) As to provision for rations: **haversack, water-bottle,** mess-tin (or billy can) with knife, fork, spoon, tin cup; 1 dry stick (towards making fire); emergency ration.

(d.) **Knapsack** containing: spare shirt, pair of socks, towel, soap, comb; scissors, needle, thread, safety-pins.

(e.) In the pocket: clasp-knife, note-book and pencil, matches in tin box, boot laces, strong cord, a candle, **coloured** handkerchiefs.

(f.) Sewn inside coat: **First Field Dressing.**

FOR OFFICERS.

(a.) As to clothes: uniform is very desirable for officers; if not worn sufficient but not unduly conspicuous distinguishing marl f rank to be worn.

(b.) . arms: **automatic pistol** or **revolver,** with **ammunition** for se e, in lieu of rifle; sword, sword bayonet, or short lance.

The rest of the equipment as for ordinary Volunteers, with the following

(c.) Additions: **Whistle** on cord; **Watch; Field Despatch-book;** Fountain Pen or **Copying-ink Pencil;** Field-Glasses; Pocket Compass; Range Finder; **Map** of District; electric torch, hooded.

Sub-Officers and **Scouts** should as far as possible be provided with the additional articles prescribed for Officers

By Order

The Equipment Order of the Irish Volunteers

The recommended kit for Irish Volunteers. The requirements could not always be fully met due to financial constraints and shortage of certain items, e.g., ammunition.

teers from all over Ireland in June 1915.

By 1916 James Connolly had himself decided to lead the Irish Citizen Army towards a Rising. His paper, the *Workers' Republic*, printed under armed guard at Liberty Hall, urged the necessity of a blow against the war. As a revolutionary socialist, Connolly had been bitterly disappointed at the failure of the international socialist movement to oppose the war, and sought to:

> set a torch to a European conflagration that will not burn out until the last throne and the last capitalist bond and debenture will be shrivelled on the funeral pyre of the last war lord.

The activities of the Citizen Army were not only of concern to the authorities. Pearse and MacNeill, of the Irish Volunteers, met Connolly to urge him not to undertake premature action; he was sceptical until Pearse made a private arrangement with him, unknown to MacNeill. On 19 January 1916, Connolly disappeared for three days of talks with the Military Council of the IRB. Agreement was reached for a united rising of the Irish Volunteers and the Citizen Army, beginning on Easter Sunday.

POLITICAL DIVISIONS AND ORGANISATIONAL FAILURES

Two considerations led to the Easter Rising being far more one-sided than anticipated by its organisers: political divisions amongst the Irish Volunteers, and the narrow failure of arms

Roger Casement was a British Consul and a known humanitarian, knighted in 1911 for his exposure of the harsh treatment of tribal people in the Congo and Peru. Casement attempted to land German arms for the Rising but was captured by the British. His high-profile trial and the release of diaries forged by the British Secret Service resulted in a death sentence. Casement was not given the benefit of a soldier's death by firing squad, but was hung in Pentonville Prison, England, in August 1916.

to arrive from Germany.

With the outbreak of the First World War a number of Irish rebels had turned to Germany in the hope that she would be willing to support an Irish insurrection. The key negotiator for the Irish was Roger Casement, an unusual figure for an Irish rebel: melancholic, upper class and holder of a British knighthood for his Foreign Service work in West Africa, which had exposed the exploitation of the native population. His mission was successful to the extent that Germany loaded a steamer, the *Aud*, with 20,000 rifles, ten machine-guns and a million rounds of ammunition. Skilfully captained by Lt Karl Spindler, the *Aud* arrived off the Kerry coast on the afternoon of 20 April. The following morning, Casement himself arrived by submarine and managed a hazardous disembarkment.

But where were the Volunteers? The British Navy was patrolling the Irish coast and it was extremely dangerous for Spindler to linger. Cruising up and down the coast, looking for a signal and a pilot, the *Aud* was finally intercepted by British warships the morning of 21 April. As he sailed with them to Queenstown Harbour [now Cobh], in County Cork, Spindler scuttled the *Aud* to prevent her valuable cargo falling into the hands of the British. Roger Casement was caught the same afternoon. German aid, which would have meant so much to the rebels, was completely wasted.

What had gone wrong? The main difficulty for the Volunteers was one of communication. While the war created the possibility of German support, it also prevented direct communication; instead the Military Council was in contact with John Devoy in New York, who was linked to the German government via the embassy

One of the Howth Mausers used by the rebels, so called because Howth was the small Dublin port used to land the consignment of rifles from Germany in July 1914.

in Washington. The rebels had finally settled on the date of Sunday, 23 April for expecting the shipment, but by the time they did so Spindler had sailed with earlier instructions. Not only that, but the British had broken the code for messages passing from Washington to Berlin.

Tragically, the local Volunteer organisation had not received

Roger Casement and the crew of U-19, the German submarine that transported Casement, Robert Monteith and Daniel Bailey to the coast of Kerry.

orders to make ready. One member remembers seeing the *Aud*:

> That evening when I went home I saw a two-masted boat about
> a mile north of Innistookert, but having no information and not
> expecting any boat until Sunday night, I took no notice of her ...
> I took her for a British decoy boat as there were many such
> around at the time.

Dublin Volunteers sent by Plunkett – almost certainly too late to
have met the *Aud* in any event – gave a further, tragic twist to the
story when their car crashed off a pier into the sea and three of
them were drowned.

Compounding this tale of mishap and disorganisation was the
existence of a split amongst the Volunteer leadership. While the
IRB members were determined to undertake the Rising, they
made up only a part of the movement. Senior Volunteer figures
such as The O'Rahilly, Bulmer Hobson, and critically, MacNeill,
the Chief of Staff, believed that military action was only permissi-
ble if there was a reasonable chance of success, or if the British
authorities gave sufficient provocation – such as by introducing
conscription or attempting to disarm the Volunteers.

FINAL CONFUSION

Despite seeking repeated assurances from his colleagues,
MacNeill was suspicious that a Rising was being planned behind
his back. On 5 April, he insisted that all orders had to be counter-
signed by him. Yet on Wednesday, 19 April all seemed changed.
Dramatic evidence appeared to indicate that the British were
about to launch a clampdown. IRB leaders produced a 'Castle
document' reporting imminent repression from the Dublin Castle
authorities. MacNeill accepted this document at face value, but he
should have been alerted by some rather strange aspects of it, not
least that it included the house arrest of Dublin's Catholic Arch-
bishop, Dr William Walsh. In fact, the document was a forgery by
the militants, designed to unite the Volunteers and to put a defen-

sive colouring on the Rising.

After heated and dramatic confrontations between the two factions amongst the leadership – with MacNeill only now discovering the plans for the Rising – it was agreed that the rebellion would take place. The split, however, re-emerged with devastating bitterness on Good Friday, just hours before the intended Rising. The IRB went so far as to kidnap Bulmer Hobson. With evidence that the *Aud* had been captured and that the 'Castle document' was a forgery, MacNeill confronted Pearse on the Saturday and demanded the Rising be halted. A crisis meeting on Sunday morning saw an unambiguous order sent out by MacNeill:

> Volunteers completely deceived. All orders for special action are hereby cancelled, and on no account will action be taken.

This was accompanied by a notice in the *Sunday Independent*, which prohibited all Volunteer movements for that day.

Those in favour of a Rising met in Liberty Hall at the same time and considered the situation. Tom Clarke argued for going ahead with the original plans, but was overruled. To give themselves time to overcome the confusion of the countermanding order, the Rising was to be put back, but only by one day. Despite the loss of the German arms and the risk that many Volunteers, especially outside Dublin, would not participate because of the countermanding order, the decision was taken to go ahead with the rebellion.

The fall-in was called for 12 noon on Easter Monday.

CHAPTER 1

OUTSIDE TRINITY COLLEGE

Trinity College faces towards Dublin Castle, seat of the governing administration for hundreds of years, and is linked to it by one of Dublin's main thoroughfares, Dame Street. Despite the importance of the street, the rebels decided not to take Trinity College due to lack of resources.

The college was established, in 1592, as an institution for a privileged Protestant élite, and this was still the case in 1916. Even as late as the 1930s, when future Minister for Health, Noel Browne, attended the medical school, he was told by a lecturer, 'no Jews or Catholics will be taught here'.

The governing body and students of Trinity united in opposition to the rebellion, and feared that they might be subject to attack. Within two hours of the beginning of the insurrection, the students had closed the doors and gates of the college and were out on the streets, pleading with Canadian and Australian soldiers to come in and defend the place of learning.

A couple of British veterans of the Boer War, then part of the Trinity Officers' Training Corps (OTC), gallantly grabbed weapons from the college armoury and stationed themselves on top of the roof of the college. They had heard that the 'Sinn Féiners' were out and were determined to relive their old war days by defending the city. Initially they caused as much trouble to the British and the citizens as they did to the rebels, as anything that moved became a legitimate target. Soon they were replaced by more 'able--bodied' medical students, at least one of whom had never even fired a weapon. Michael Taffe, an inquisitive scholar who had heard gunshots from his home, rushed to the College to find himself 'volunteered' by an old war-horse into manning the roof. He claimed more hits against the opposite building than the opposite side.

Across College Green from Trinity is the Bank of Ireland building, which once housed the Irish Parliament. The rebels did not take this building, despite its political symbolism, but it is worth drawing attention to this as it highlights one of the rebellion's main aims. Ireland's only previous experience with a very limited form of self-government was from 1782 to the abolition of the Dublin Parliament in 1800. However, the Irish Parliament was tightly connected to the ruling Protestant ascendancy; Catholics could not vote until 1793, let alone serve in parliament. Even Protestants such as Henry Grattan, who had taken inspiration from the American Declaration of Independence (1776) and had campaigned for increased self-government in Ireland, were nevertheless afraid that Catholic emancipation might threaten their property. Ultimately the parliament proved unwilling to challenge British authority. The Irish Parliament became that rare creature, a parliament in which the politicians voted themselves out of a job, when it followed the wishes of Westminster and dissolved itself prior to the Act of Union of 1801.

The declaration of a Provisional Irish Government, based at the rebel headquarters at the GPO, was the first time since 1800 that Ireland had had its own government, and prefigured the days of 1919, when – this time with mass democratic support behind it – the first Dáil Éireann (Irish Parliament) was set up.

In 1916 the building functioned as a bank and thus was well-defended by guards who would be unwilling to allow armed men inside. The rebels also favoured buildings with windows, which they could break and barricade, giving themselves a clear position from which to prepare for British attacks. It does not take a military genius to see that there are no windows in the Bank of Ireland (because of a window tax); for the purposes of the insurrection this rendered the building useless.

At the time of the Rising there was a statue of King William III (1650–1702), known as William of Orange, on College Green in front of Trinity and to the left of the Bank of Ireland. This statue has been replaced by a fountain, representing freedom; 'King Billy' and his horse were blown up in 1929. This rearrangement of the statues provides a good visual symbol of the differences between the old and the new – differences which were represented in the rebellion.

In College Green there is also a statue of Thomas Davis (1814–1845), well remembered for his contribution to the cause of Irish freedom. The songs of Davis were an inspiration to Pearse and the other insurrectionists. Whenever morale flagged, the words of 'A Nation Once Again' echoed from the rebel positions, a poignant reminder to the Volunteers that they were part of a long tradition of Irish aspiration for independence. Even though the chances of success were negligible, these songs at least gave a sense of history and courage to the rebels.

A NATION ONCE AGAIN

When boyhood's fire was in my blood
I read of ancient freemen.
For Greece and Rome who bravely stood,
Three hundred men and three men.
And then I prayed I might yet see,
Our fetters rent in twain,
And Ireland, long a province, be
A Nation once again!

Chorus:

A Nation once again,
A Nation once again,
And Ireland, long a province, be
A Nation once again

And from that time, through wildest woe,
That hope has shone a far light,
Nor could love's brightest summer glow
Outshine that solemn starlight;
It seemed to watch above my head
In forum, field and fane,
Its angel voice sang round my bed
A Nation once again!

Repeat Chorus

It whisper'd too, that freedom's ark
And service high and holy
Would be profaned by feelings dark
And passions vain or lowly;
For Freedom comes from God's right hand,
And needs a godly train;
And righteous men must make our land
A Nation once again!

Repeat Chorus

So, as I grew from boy to man
I bent me to that bidding.
My spirit of each selfish plan
And cruel passion ridding.
For thus I hoped some day to aid,
Oh, can such hope be vain?
When my dear country shall be made
A Nation once again!

Repeat Chorus

Thomas Davis (1814–1845)

DEFENCE OF TCD

The soldiers brought in to defend Trinity College took up a position in the corner tower of the front buildings from where they could fire upon the main rebel position in Sackville Street [O'Connell Street]. For the week of the Rising, a long-range sniping duel took place between these impromptu defenders of Trinity and the rebels. The defenders were able to count themselves lucky as the rebels made no attempt to take their position. The young students had even 'bagged a Shinner', as an unlucky messenger on his way to rebel HQ on a bicycle had fallen foul of a sniper's bullet. The British Army was soon in a position to take over the defence of this part of the city. Sadly, from the rebels' viewpoint, they had also missed an opportunity to commandeer at least 300 rifles and a few thousand rounds of ammunition from the stock belonging to the OTC. By 12 noon on Tuesday, with a machine-gun placed on top of the roof, Trinity was almost impenetrable.

In fact, as Trinity was so well defended, Brigadier-General W.H.M. Lowe of the Reserve Cavalry made it his headquarters when he arrived in Dublin from the Curragh, in County Kildare, to quell the rebellion. Lowe arrived at daybreak on Tuesday morning with a mobile force of 1,500 dismounted cavalry, which swelled the number of British troops to nearly 5,000. In effect, the rebels were outnumbered after the first day by four to one, and more troops were on their way from England.

The General's immediate plan was to throw cordons of British soldiers around rebel positions and strangle them into submission. Until he was sure of the scale of the insurrection, General Lowe decided to move cautiously. His plans of containment and gradual encroachment were described by an Irish military historian, Colonel Hally, as 'sound, and they paid off in results'.

The rebels had been gambling on this approach. They needed time to communicate their actions to the country and indeed Europe. They hoped that as news of their action spread, many of those who had previously dismissed the Irish Volunteers as play-actors would rally to them. Some rebels also hoped that the Irish regiments still in the country might mutiny and take the side of the Rising.

Lt-General Sir John Maxwell and his entourage inspect British troops after the Rising.

By contrast, the commander appointed to take charge of the British forces, Lt-General Sir John Maxwell, carried out a far more aggressive strategy from his arrival at the North Wall, Dublin, at 2am on Friday, 28 April. Maxwell had recently been withdrawn from Egypt due to reorganisation, and had returned to England just three weeks before the Rising. The widespread use of the incendiary devices and heavy artillery that caused so much damage to the city was a feature of his determination to root out the rebels.

Maxwell issued the following proclamation on his arrival:

> Most rigorous measures will be taken by me to stop the loss of life and damage to property which certain misguided persons are causing by their armed resistance to the law. If necessary, I shall not hesitate to destroy all buildings within any area occupied by rebels, and I warn all persons within the area specified below, and now surrounded by His Majesty's troops, forthwith to leave such area under the following conditions:

(a) women and children may leave the area from any of the examining posts set up for the purpose, and will be allowed to go away free;

(b) men may leave by the same examining posts, and will be allowed to go away free, provided the examining officer is satisfied they have taken no part whatever in the present disturbances; all other men who present themselves at the said examining posts must surrender unconditionally, together with any arms and ammunition in their possession.

This General is remembered as 'Bloody' Maxwell, as it was under his orders that the leaders of the Rising were executed. As it transpired, he made a grave error in pursuing the death penalty for the rebel leaders. This policy led directly to the creation of martyrs.

SOUTH DUBLIN UNION

If you look to the southwest on the map you will see the site of the most bitter and grim fighting in the Rising. At the time, the South Dublin Union (originally a workhouse) was a complex of buildings spread over fifty acres, including two churches, residences, a poorhouse and a hospital. As it was protected on two sides by the Grand Canal, and contained its own bakery, the Fourth Dublin Battalion, led by Commandant Eamonn Ceannt, hoped to se-

Eamonn Ceannt was an uileann piper, a member of the IRB Military Council and a signatory of the Proclamation. He was stationed in South Dublin Union during the Rising and was executed in Kilmainham Gaol on 8 May 1916.

cure the area for some time. However, the small turnout of Volunteers meant that the garrison was soon in difficulties.

One survivor remembers that British soldiers swiftly penetrated the area and cut off a number of Volunteers:

> With our men scattered all over the place and with the enemy literally in our midst the situation was an ugly one. It was like hide and seek and many encounters took place at point blank range.

Indeed, mortal injuries were inflicted by rifle butt and bayonet. Long chases down dark corridors and sudden encounters resulted in civilian casualties. Nurse Keogh, who had stayed to guard inmates of the hospital, was shot dead by British soldiers.

An extraordinary incident took place when, overestimating the force against them, the rebels retreated from a critical barricade guarding the way into the nurses' home. The little garrison had been awaiting their final defeat for some two hours when they suddenly heard the sound of British grenades and, in reply, the bark of a rebel Mauser. Then, above the din, could be heard someone singing 'God save Ireland'. A scout sent back to the barricade found that it was being defended by Cathal Brugha. He had been wounded by a grenade and many bullets and was lying in a pool of blood which had spread to four feet around his body. Cathal Brugha had revived with the return of the British troops and had held the position alone. The effect of his resistance was electric and the Volunteers, led by Commandant Ceannt, rushed back to clear the nurses' home.

Despite the bitterness of this confrontation, it was not without humorous incidents, for example, the embarrassment of Volunteers as they carried off armfuls of nurses' clothes from the home – with the intention of filling them with clay for barricades.

After one daring charge towards the bakehouse by four British soldiers, all of them fell, apparently dead. In fact, two of the soldiers, still alive, lay stiffly for hours under the direct gaze of the rebels. Later, when nurses came to remove the bodies, they took pity on the two soldiers who made a sensational escape by coffin. The hearses were led away through rebel-held grounds until they

Irish Rebellion. May 1916.
Soldiers holding a Dublin Street.

The rebels utilised whatever material was available to erect impromptu barricades such as this one. This photograph of British troops is obviously staged as one soldier has left his backpack on the wrong side of the fortification.

reached the nearby suburb of Rialto, directly south of the Union. There, much to the consternation of passers-by, the hearses stopped and out of two of the coffins leapt the British soldiers.

THE MAGAZINE FORT IN THE PHOENIX PARK

Thirty men gathered for a game of football on top of Thomas's Hill in the Phoenix Park at precisely 12.17pm – a perfectly innocent activity under normal circumstances. However, the Magazine Fort, a British Army arsenal, was situated on top of the same hill and these 'footballers' were all Irish Volunteers, whose task it was to blow up the building as a signal that the Rising had begun. Paddy Daly had mobilised his men in quite a rush that Easter Monday morning. His comrade, Garry Holohan, barely had time to gather his thoughts when Daly woke him from his slumber to let him know that the Rising was to go ahead despite the countermanding order. While Daly went about town in an attempt to gather more men, Holohan found Volunteer Tim Roche and ordered him to commandeer an escape vehicle from the Phoenix Park.

As the football game progressed, the ball seemed to find its way nearer to the Magazine Fort with each kick. Suddenly, the Volunteer sportsmen pounced upon the unsuspecting sentry who had eyed the game with bemusement. The rebels then charged inside the Fort, taking as many small arms as they could find and disarming the British soldiers at gunpoint.

Holohan placed five bags of gelignite against the wall of the explosives storeroom and set the fuses alight. Everyone was ordered to evacuate, including the Playfair family whose quarters were attached to the Fort. Rebels, British soldiers and civilians streamed down the hill expecting an explosion within minutes.

Volunteer Roche waited in the getaway vehicle, not a motorcar as expected but a horse-drawn hansom cab, much to the annoyance of Daly who wanted to remove himself from the area as quickly as possible.

As the horse galloped off in the direction of the city centre, the Volunteers noticed a terrified figure dashing towards a constable on traffic duty. It was the eldest Playfair boy, whose father was fighting in France at the time, and who perhaps felt it was his duty to raise the alarm. Without hesitation Garry Holohan, who had been cycling behind the horse and carriage, gave chase on his old bicycle. Young Playfair seemed to think it safer to head for a nearby house rather than the protection of the policeman. Just as the seventeen-year-old made it to the doorway, Holohan took aim with his revolver and shot the boy three times.

While Playfair lay dying in the half-opened doorway of a stranger's house, the gelignite in the Fort exploded. Rather than a huge boom, the explosion was more like a dull thud. As a signal for the Rising to begin this action was, therefore, a failure, but as a tactical move the rebels could at least derive satisfaction from the partial destruction of the Magazine Fort.

CORNER OF SACKVILLE ST. & EDEN QUAY DUBLIN.

CHANCELLOR, DUB

Above: Daniel O'Connell looks out on a spectacular view of the ruined city of Dublin.

Below: Crowds are kept back from buildings tottering on the brink of collapse.

CHAPTER 2

PEARSE STREET

Standing on Dublin's Pearse Street [formerly Great Brunswick Street], one is reminded that there are many streets and buildings named after the participants of the 1916 Rising. Gone are the old names of British politicians, generals and admirals, replaced by the names of those who are considered to have helped achieve Irish independence, and especially the prominent figures from 1916. This busy thoroughfare is, of course, named after the first Provisional President of the Irish Republic, and the Pearses's old house can be found at number 27. Pádraic Pearse was the main orator and literary voice of the rebellion. He had joined the Gaelic League in 1895 and had become the editor of its newspaper, *An Claidheamh Soluis*, in 1903. To implement his belief in the importance of an Irish education for Irish children, he founded St Enda's school in 1908, a radical institution not only for its advocacy of Irish culture, but also for its egalitarian outlook and avoidance of clerical control.

> I do not grudge them; Lord, I do not grudge
> My two strong sons that I have seen go out
> To break their strength and die, they and a few,
> In bloody protest for a glorious thing.
>
> Pádraic Pearse, 'The Mother'

Pearse had become disillusioned with the constitutional approach to national independence and, fired by the belief that Britain was in the process of betraying the country, he began to speak out in favour of militant republicanism. His finest hour as a speaker

P.H. Pearse was an intellectual, a poet, an educator, a visionary,
a member of the IRB Military Council and a signatory of the Proclamation.
He was President of the Provisional Government and was stationed in the GPO during
the Rising. Pearse was executed in Kilmainham Gaol on 3 May 1916.

came at the funeral of O'Donovan Rossa, that 'unrepentant Fenian', in 1915, where Pearse concluded sombrely and powerfully:

> Life springs from death; and from the graves of patriot men and women spring living nations. The Defenders of this Realm have worked well in secret and in the open. They think that they have pacified Ireland. They think that they have purchased half of us and intimidated the other half. They think they have foreseen everything, think they have provided against everything; but the fools, the fools, the fools! they have left us our Fenian dead, and while Ireland holds these graves, Ireland unfree shall never be at peace.

Pearse was President of the Provisional Government created by the Rising and Commander-in-Chief of the rebel force, although he left the practical side of the operations in Dublin to Connolly. It was Pearse who read aloud, on the steps of the GPO, the Proclamation that he had helped compose, and to him fell the heavy responsibility of agreeing to surrender to the British authorities. He was the first leader to be executed, four days after the Rising.

In addition to the renaming of streets and buildings, one of the

NA FIANNA ÉIREANN

In August 1909, Countess Markievicz and Bulmer Hobson, an IRB revivalist, organised the nationalist youth into Na Fianna Éireann (Warriors of Ireland). Na Fianna were the standing army and bodyguards of Ireland during the time of the mythological hero Fionn Mac Cumhaill. The idea behind the modern Fianna was to encourage the boys to study their heritage and culture, thus developing their sense of nationalism and independence. Military drills were held alongside sporting events and Hobson's influence is clear when one considers that many of these 'boy scouts' went on to become fully fledged members of the Irish Republican Brotherhood. For example, one of the rebels who met with execution, Con Colbert, had been trained through the Fianna – during the Rising he led a small contingent of Volunteers in Watkin's Brewery, Ardee Street.

highest accolades given to rebel fighters was to have train stations named in their honour. In Dublin, for example, you find Pearse Street Station, Connolly Station and Heuston Station.

The story behind the naming of Heuston Station is that of Seán Heuston, a young Fianna Éireann Volunteer. He was given the task of commanding the Mendicity Institution, a poorhouse on the quays. With a handful of Fianna scouts between the ages of twelve and sixteen, he was instructed to hold his position for two

The five young members of the Fianna Éireann Council pictured in 1915.
Seated on the far right is Cornelius 'Con' Colbert, wearing the uniform of Na Fianna.
-ing the Rising, Captain Colbert, IRB member of the Volunteers' Committee, was given the
-sk of seizing Watkin's Brewery in Ardee Street. Colbert was a young man of twenty-three
when he was executed in Kilmainham Gaol on 8 May 1916.

hours to delay British deployment into the city, while the rest of the battalions settled into their given areas. When the two hours were up, all the boys decided to remain in the Mendicity Institution, rather than go home as ordered.

Even though they only had two weapons and one box of ammunition, these children remained fast in their building for three days. They received thirteen reinforcements from the North Country Battalion, but coming under intense fire from the British and vastly out-numbered they were forced to surrender on the Wednesday of the Rising – with two of their troop dead. The

Seán Heuston was the young Commandant who took over the Mendicity Institution. He was executed in Kilmainham Gaol on 8 May 1916.

British soldiers were disgusted when they realised that they had been held back so long by such a small (and young) force.

The fact that Heuston and his boys were holding their post soon became known to the other battalions and their example boosted the morale of the other rebel fighters. For this command, nineteen-year-old Heuston was shot dead in Kilmainham Gaol, Maxwell refusing any leniency for his youth. The twenty-three other young rebel survivors were all sentenced to between eighteen and twenty-five years in jail. The nearby Kingsbridge Station was thus renamed in 1966 in honour of Heuston and his garrison.

In a south Dublin suburb called Kimmage, about three miles from the city centre, Joseph Plunkett lived with his family. His father, Count Plunkett, had invited Irishmen living in England to return home and avoid conscription into the British Army. Over a period of a few months, about fifty to sixty men, including the

relatively unknown Michael Collins, took up the Plunkett offer of
board, lodgings and military training. These men lived and
breathed insurrection. Their daily routines centred around preparations for a rising. They constructed home-made pikes and
bombs. A more ambitious attempt to construct a type of machine-
gun, by filling a piece of iron drainpipe with gunpowder and bits of
metal, was ended when it exploded prematurely, nearly killing
their hosts. But in general the existence of the 'rebel farm' was
greatly appreciated by those planning the Rising, as can be under-
stood when one considers how little weaponry was available to
the insurrectionists.

On the morning of the rebellion, Easter Monday, fifty-six men

JOSEPH PLUNKETT

The son of a papal count and a distinguished national scholar,
Joseph Plunkett became a radical nationalist in his own right, joining
the IRB through his involvement in Irish arts. Plunkett was a poet, a
director of the Hardwicke Street Theatre and for a time he edited the
Irish Review.

marched out of the Kimmage
farm. The time was 10am and
the 'Kimmage Men', as they
were known, were intent on
reaching Liberty Hall on
Eden Quay for the noon dead-
line that was to mark the
start of the rebellion. The
weather was warm and the
men were carrying heavy
supplies and weapons, both
for themselves and for their
comrades in the city centre.
The fifty-seventh member of
this group was George

Joseph Plunkett working on wireless equipment.

Captain Michael Collins, ADC to Joseph Plunkett during the Rising, where he fought in the GPO. He rose to greater prominence during the Anglo-Irish War of Independence (1919–1921).

Plunkett, Joseph's brother, leading his men into the city. After a mile of marching they reached the south Dublin suburb of Harold's Cross, where the tired rebels saw an open-top tram on its way into town. With a general sigh of relief, the troop hailed the tram and made to get on. Both driver and passengers were alarmed at the appearance of so many armed men and the driver hesitated. In what has become a legendary gesture, George asked for fifty-seven tuppenny fares. The troops finished their journey in great spirits, singing nationalist airs.

This polite behaviour was not unusual for a Plunkett, as the family took pride in honesty. There are many other stories of the rebels being unwilling to take financial advantage of their arms, thus bearing out the repeated promises of the leaders that the reputation of the Irish Republic would not be sullied by stealing or looting. It was common for officers to issue chits, 'redeemable by the Irish Republic', for such food and materials as were commandeered. Most of these were lost or discarded, probably with a measure of disgust. Ironically, they would be worth a great deal today. In this context, when rebel officer Lt Joseph O'Byrne took over the doctor's house at Boland's Bakery (where the Grand Canal meets the Liffey), he found half a dozen gold sovereigns on top of a desk. He promptly locked them in the desk drawer and left a note informing their owner of the gold's whereabouts. Similarly, Liam Ó Briain, a lecturer in Romance languages and a Volunteer, wrote a note apologising to a houseowner whose door was pickaxed and barricaded: 'I hope you approve of the cause.' At Westland Row Station [now Pearse Street Station], hungry Volunteers preferred to take up a collection of small change for the chocolate and cigarette machines rather than break into them.

The outstanding physical feature that dominates this spot on Pearse Street, even today, is the redbrick lookout tower of the nearby Fire Brigade station (Tara Street). A British machine-gunner was stationed in this strategic position during the rebellion. In 1916 the large grey government buildings were not present and this soldier had a very clear line of fire down to the quays. His sights were trained on the door of Liberty Hall in preparation for the proposed bombardment of that building.

Here also is the grey granite building of Pearse Street Garda Station, formerly belonging to the Dublin Metropolitan Police (DMP). The DMP were generally very quick to leave the streets of Dublin during the rebellion. They feared that Connolly's Citizen Army would be seeking revenge for their ill treatment in the great Lockout of 1913. Their fears were misplaced, as there was no attempt to search out DMP men for retaliation.

The first death during the Rising was, however, that of a policeman: Constable James O'Brien, a Dubliner, was shot at around 12pm by the rebels when he refused to leave his post outside Dublin Castle.

When Commandant Edward Daly, from his position at the Four Courts, raided the Bridewell police station, he discovered to his amusement that for their own safety the police had moved the prisoners and hidden themselves inside the cells.

Bowen-Colthurst's Madness

Francis Sheehy Skeffington was a well-known character in Dublin, a pacifist, a women's rights campaigner, a vegetarian, an anti-conscription advocate and, amongst other things, a gentleman. 'Skeffy' organised soup kitchens for the hungry during the infamous Lockout of 1913. He even resigned his position as Provost of University College, Dublin over its refusal to allow women study for degrees. With his wife, Hanna, he was a tireless champion of the underdog. To Sheehy Skeffington, the underdogs during the Rising were the shopowners whose premises were being looted by the public after the Dublin Metropolitan Police were withdrawn. He decided that he would form a temporary citizen's police force of his own. His manifesto said:

> When there are no regular police on the streets, it becomes the duty of the citizens to police the streets themselves – to prevent such spasmodic looting as has taken place in a few streets. Citizens (men and women) who are willing to co-operate to this end are asked to attend at Westmoreland Chambers at five o'clock this Tuesday afternoon.

Understandably, there were no volunteers for this force and Sheehy Skeffington was unable single-handedly to stop the looting. On his way home from the GPO, where he had insisted on a meeting with the sympathetic Connolly, he was arrested as a 'Shinner' by the military. He was taken to Portobello Barracks and held for some time, until a certain Captain J. Bowen-Colthurst decided that the prisoner would make an ideal human shield.

With Sheehy Skeffington as a 'safety net', Bowen-Colthurst and a few privates went to Rathmines, a suburb of the city, to see what mischief could be performed. Martial law had been declared some hours earlier, but a young man of seventeen, J.J. Coade, was returning from Mass unaware of the curfew. Bowen-Colthurst shot him at point blank range immediately after a private had bashed Coade in the face with a rifle butt.

In Rathmines there was a pub owned by Alderman James Kelly, who was unlucky enough to share a name with a Sinn Féin councillor. Bowen-Colthurst had his men bomb this pub and forcibly remove the occupants, two barmen and two loyalist magazine editors, Patrick MacIntyre and Thomas Dickson. All four were taken back to Portobello Barracks along with Sheehy Skeffington. The newspapermen protested that they were not rebels of any sort, and indeed had both been involved in the recruitment campaign to encourage Irishmen to volunteer for the war against Germany. Their protestations fell upon deaf ears as Bowen-Colthurst had now become agitated and unreasonable to the point where his own men were in fear of him.

The next morning, Wednesday, Bowen-Colthurst ordered that Sheehy Skeffington, MacIntyre and Dickson were to be brought out to a yard and shot by firing squad. Sheehy Skeffington was only wounded by some of the bullets from the seven-man firing squad, and a British soldier had to return to finish the job. The bodies of the murdered men were buried in quicklime to hide the evidence, a fact that suggests that Bowen-Colthurst knew quite well that he had performed an illegal act. Furthermore, he was not even of high enough rank in the barracks to issue such orders. But there was no one to stop him.

Councillor Richard O'Carroll was also unfortunate enough to fall into the hands of this officer on the Wednesday. O'Carroll was asked was he a Sinn Féiner, to which he promptly replied, 'from the backbone out'. Richard O'Carroll was then shot, dying nine days later in Portobello Hospital.

Bowen-Colthurst belonged to an aristocratic family, was a veteran of the Boer War and had once been ADC to Lord Aberdeen, the Viceroy before Lord Wimborne. One British officer, Major Sir Francis Fletcher Vane, did later demand that Bowen-Colthurst be arrested after he heard that the Captain had killed at least six people. As Second-in-Command in Portobello he spoke to the officer in charge there, Major James Rossborough, who reluctantly confined Bowen-Colthurst to barracks. The subsequent promotion of Bowen-Colthurst and the attempted bribery of Hanna Sheehy Skeffington played an important part in changing Irish public opinion after the Rising (*see* Chapter 9).

Nothing spreads like a rumour in times of upheaval, and it was not long before the dogs in the streets were whispering that Sheehy Skeffington had been shot.

This rumour paled into insignificance when one considers the half truths and downright lies that were being spread around town. Given that there were no newspapers (the *Mail* and *Express* offices were under the command of the rebels and *The Irish Times* building was off limits), it was left to the fertile imagination of Dubliners to spread the news as they saw it. The most outlandish rumours were that the Pope had committed suicide, King George V had been captured by the rebels, and the Germans had landed not one but 100 submarines in the pond in St Stephen's Green. Whatever about the Pope and the U-boats, we can trace the origin of the rumour concerning the King. The GPO rebels had 'commandeered' a couple of effigies from the waxworks, one of Lord Kitchener and the other of King George. Kitchener, whose famous face was synonymous with the recruitment posters of this period, was propped up in the GPO and used for target practice by inkbottle throwers. To the amusement of the garrison, the King was unmajestically used to prop up a barricade, thus helping to sustain the rumour that he had, indeed, been captured.

CHAPTER 3

BUTT BRIDGE

Butt Bridge is named after Isaac Butt, one of Ireland's first political figures to raise the issue of Home Rule in Westminster. Butt, a Protestant lawyer, led a rather disorganised Irish faction of MPs during the early 1870s. His efforts indicate that not all moves towards independence were necessarily based on Catholic nationalist ideas. Back in the 1870s many of Ireland's ruling class believed that they could govern themselves better than a government based in Westminster.

The Custom House, overshadowed somewhat by the Loop Line Railway Bridge from behind which the *Helga* fired at Liberty Hall. This picture was taken immediately after the Rising.

Facing east you can see the docks, beyond which lie Dublin Bay, the Irish Sea and eventually Wales. On the left is the magnificent Custom House – during the Rising it was used by the army as a launch point for an attack on Liberty Hall on the quays, and later as a depot for prisoners. Built to the design of James Gandon, and completed in 1791, the Custom House is somewhat overshadowed by the ugly monstrosity of the Loop Line Railway Bridge, constructed during Ireland's industrial revolution. Four years after the Rising, during the War of Independence, the Custom House was subject to an arson attack, to destroy the records it contained, under the orders of Éamon de Valera. During the 1916 Rising, Éamon de Valera was the Commandant of the Third Battalion. His survival as one of the more senior rebels in the aftermath of the rebellion brought him to a public prominence which he never lost. De Valera would later found the Fianna Fáil (soldiers of destiny) Party and would be a key figure in Irish political life for decades.

Mount Street Bridge

Winding southbound the Loop Line comes to Boland's Bakery (see southeast on the map). During the Rising this was the HQ of Éamon de Valera and the Volunteers' Third Battalion. Part of his command were posted at Mount Street Bridge, scene of the fiercest battle of the rebellion. In what has often been described as the Irish Thermopylae, fifteen men under George Reynolds, a unit commander whose wedding was scheduled for the following week, and Michael Malone took over three posts at the bridge over the Grand Canal. Malone, a carpenter and member of the Volunteers cyclists' section, took charge of troop positions. To give themselves full command of the route to the south, from Dún Laoghaire harbour to Dublin, Clanwilliam House and 25 Northumberland Road were also seized.

Shortly after the Rising began, at 2.30pm, a cyclist in civilian clothes reached Dún Laoghaire [Kingstown] military base and a telegram was sent to the Admiralty via Liverpool. Communication between British forces and their HQ was severely disrupted the following morning when power to the base failed, leaving the radio on the HMS *Adventure* as the only link to Britain. However, the early signal had been sufficient.

The British authorities moved quickly, commandeering the Ulster mail steamer and directing it to transfer the 178th Brigade 'Sherwood Foresters' to Ireland. On the Wednesday of the Rising, the Sherwood Foresters arrived at Dún

A house on Clanwilliam Place, riddled with bullet holes, shows the ferocity of the battle of Mount Street Bridge.

Laoghaire as the first major contingent of British reinforcements. These soldiers were warmly greeted by the local citizens and were offered tea and sandwiches, which were refused in case they were poisoned. The soldiers were raw recruits, some only sixteen or seventeen years old, who thought they were in France for the war, greeting any young ladies with a hearty 'Bonjour, Mademoiselle'.

The British reinforcements divided into two columns, one reaching its Kilmainham destination without difficulty. But the other, marching into town via Ballsbridge, suffered the worst casualties of the conflict. By the time they arrived at Mount Street the Sherwood Foresters were tired and probably did not expect the barrage of fire that opened upon their ranks. The soldiers' lack of training led many of them to their deaths, as they blindly persisted in a costly frontal assault, but the rebels' superior positioning and basic determination were the real reasons for the astonishing number of casualties inflicted upon the British at Mount Street Bridge.

Mick Malone had positioned himself and his companion, James Grace, at the upper windows of 25 Northumberland Road to cover just such a march of reinforcements from Dún Laoghaire.

Six other rebels with George Reynolds in nearby Clanwilliam House added their firepower to obstruct the Foresters. Caught between two fires and uncertain as to their source, the British strayed from line of fire to line of fire and casualties began to mount. Repeated attempts by officers to lead bayonet charges of fifty to sixty men petered out in the face of blistering shooting from the rebels. Eventually, after five hours of fighting the rebels ran out of ammunition and the British were able to take Mount Street Bridge and secure the road into town. But the cost had been horrific: 216 soldiers dead or wounded, fourteen officers wounded, four killed. On the rebel side casualties were surprisingly few. Mick Malone died, smoking his pipe, shot while coming down the stairs of number 25, but his companion, James Grace, survived, having been missed in a search while he hid behind a cooker. Three rebels in Clanwilliam House, including the commanding officer George Reynolds, were shot dead. If such had been the general pattern of resistance the rebellion would have been able to mount a protracted defence against the British army. However, not all the soldiers were as inexperienced, nor all the rebel positions so ideally placed.

LIBERTY HALL

> For many years past Liberty Hall has been a thorn in the side of the
> Dublin Police and the Irish Government. It was the centre of social
> anarchy in Ireland, the brain of every riot and disturbance.
>
> *The Irish Times*, 1916

At the east end of Eden Quay stands Liberty Hall, currently
Dublin's tallest building at sixteen stories high. Some say this is
in memory of 1916 and others maintain it is to commemorate
each of the sixteen men who were executed as a result of the rebellion. The existing building is founded on the ruins of the
two-story Liberty Hall that was the headquarters of the Irish
Transport and General Workers' Union in 1916.

Before the rebellion, James Connolly had stretched a huge
banner across Liberty Hall. The banner was white with bold black
lettering stating:

WE SERVE NEITHER KING NOR KAISER BUT IRELAND

This was displayed in answer to those who were maintaining that
Connolly and other revolutionary nationalists were in the pay of
Germany – fighting British rule not out of principle, but for gain.

Liberty Hall was a thorn in the side of the British authorities
and Irish employers alike. Its halls and rooms were given over to a
multitude of workers' groups and nationalist organisations. If a
raid was expected, the Irish Citizen Army would be on hand to
stand guard.

In the basement of the building was a printing press, the source
of much of Dublin's subversive literature. It was to this printer that
the Proclamation was brought, the text having been settled by the
seven signatories on Easter Sunday. Compositors Christopher Brady,
Liam Ó Briain and Michael Molloy had to struggle to find sufficient
letters, with different fonts and even sealing wax being required to
complete the document. It is generally thought that Pearse was the

first person to read the Proclamation aloud, but, in fact, Countess Markievicz eagerly grabbed the first of the run of 1,000 as it came off the press and read it out to those outside Liberty Hall.

Liberty Hall, headquarters of the Irish Transport and General Workers' Union (ITGWU) and the Irish Citizen Army. The banner served to remind citizens of the harsh treatment meted out to disobedient subjects of the British Empire.

At 8am on Wednesday morning, the third day of the rebellion, a gunboat called the *Helga* sailed up the Liffey and anchored beside the Custom House. She was an antisubmarine vessel, based in Dún Laoghaire. Two Irishmen in her crew risked their careers, and indeed lives, by refusing to serve on her against the rebels. The British plan was to remove the hundreds of rebels they believed were stationed in the building by bombarding them out and mowing them down. Backed up by the machine-gunner positioned on the Fire Brigade tower in Tara Street, various 'squaddies' crouched down behind the quay walls with their rifles trained on Liberty Hall, waiting for the signal to fire.

The first shot from the *Helga*'s three-foot gun was aimed directly at Liberty Hall, but smacked into the Loop Line Bridge, ricocheting back past the ship with a metallic whine that was heard right across the city centre. Only when the artillery crew changed tactics and tried arcing their fire over the bridge was the building hit. After the first artillery shell landed on top of the roof of Liberty Hall, the side door opened and the solitary occupant, the old caretaker, Peter Ennis, came out as if to enquire who was knocking. There was a hail of gunfire from all quarters. Ennis ran for his life down Eden Quay, bullets tearing up the pavement around his heels. He felt that the whole British Army was after him. Luck was with him that morning for he escaped into a crowd of onlookers and became a legend as one of Ireland's greatest sprinters – eyewitnesses claimed he completed the 100-yard dash in less than ten seconds. A reporter, John O'Leary, sitting at a window, wrote down his observation of the event:

> Suddenly, amid the roar of the field gun and the whizz of the Maxim's bullets, a Sinn Féiner emerges from a side door and dashes wildly up Eden Quay. A machine gun is turned on him. Bullets hit the pavement in front of him and behind him, they strike the roadway and the walls of the buildings along his route, and still he runs on and on. I hold my breath in awe as I watch his mad career. Will he escape? He will – he won't. 'My God!' I exclaim as a bullet raises a spark from the pavement right at his toe. A hundred yards in nine seconds – a record! Nonsense, this man does the distance in five …

It was the intention of the rebel leaders to leave Liberty Hall empty and their decision proved to be wise. The *Helga* continued to bombard an empty building for more than two hours, wasting ammunition and valuable time. Then she sailed down to the Grand Canal Docks on the south side of Dublin. The crew was given a new order, to train their big guns on Boland's Bakery, occupied by

Éamon de Valera, Volunteer Commander in Boland's Bakery during the
Rising and destined to become Taoiseach (Prime Minister) and
President of the Republic of Ireland.

Commandant Éamon de Valera. When the first few artillery shells landed, 'Dev', or 'The Long Fella' as he was nicknamed, ordered his men to hoist a green flag on top of a distillery tower to deflect the fire away from their immediate position. The *Helga*'s gunner of course began to aim for the flag, but the shots were sallying past it and landing near the British troops who were attempting to bombard the rebels out of Clanwilliam House at Mount Street Bridge, using portable cannons called howitzers. The British thought that the rebels had heavy weapons and began to return fire in the direction the shells had come from. Before the mistake was realised, howitzer shots had flown back over Dev's position and three of them landed so close to the *Helga* that the gun crew were actually soaked.

The flags used by the rebels included other designs. In particular, 1916 was the first time that the tricolour was flown from public buildings in Ireland. This flag was one of the few lasting gains from the Young Ireland movement of 1848. In that year revolution had broken out all over Europe as emerging nations and republics struggled against empire and aristocracy. The very name Young Ireland was an adaptation of the name used by the Italian revolutionary Mazzini for the revolutionary association, Young Italy, which he founded in 1831. The tricolour of green, white and orange (to symbolise the unity of Catholic and Protestant) was a gift from revolutionary Europe and was subsequently adopted as the flag of the Irish nation.

BOLAND'S BAKERY

De Valera's role as a commander is a highly controversial one. Although his flag ruse was effective, some of his other decisions were not so productive. Many writers have wondered why he did not reinforce Mick Malone at Clanwilliam House. For the bulk of his men, the main strain came not from fighting but from the anticipation of action and from lack of sleep. De Valera allowed himself very little sleep and perhaps that explains his contradictory behaviour. He

THE HISTORY OF THE IRISH FLAG

The origin of the Irish tricolour is in the history of the early nineteenth century and it is emblematic of the fusion of the older elements, represented by the green, with the newer elements, represented by the orange. The combination of both colours in the tricolour, with the white between in token of brotherhood, symbolises the union of the different stocks, Catholic and Protestant, in a common nationality.

In March 1848, Irish tricolours appeared side by side with French ones at meetings held all over France to celebrate the revolution that had just then taken place. In April, Thomas Francis Meagher, the Young Ireland leader, brought a silk tricolour of orange, white and green from Paris and presented it to a Dublin meeting. John Mitchel, Young Irelander and founder of radical newspaper, United Irishmen, referring to it, said: 'I hope to see that flag one day waving as our national banner.'

At that time, however, and for long afterwards, the national flag was green with a yellow or gold harp. Although the tricolour was not forgotten as a symbol of union and as a banner associated with the Young Irelanders, it was little used between 1848 and 1916. Even up to the eve of the Rising in 1916, the green flag with the gold harp held undisputed sway.

Flown over the GPO during the Rising, the tricolour was soon acclaimed throughout the country as the national flag. It continued to be recognised by official usage during the period 1922–1937, when its position as the national flag was formally confirmed by the Constitution, Article 7 of which states: 'The national flag is the tricolour of green, white and orange.'

planned to capture a train and drive it through British lines, only to call off the manoeuvre at the last moment. He had the equally inspired idea of relieving Michael Mallin, the Citizen Army Commandant based at St Stephen's Green, by sending a party into the Shelbourne Hotel from its rear, for which a volunteer party was assembled before it too was cancelled. He also ordered the firing of Westland Row, only to change his mind and have the same men put the fire out.

Since the Boland's Bakery area was so well secured, de Valera's men refused to surrender even after being presented with the order. It took long negotiations before the surrender was complete and many men broke their rifles on the ground rather than give them up.

De Valera was extremely fortunate to survive the aftermath of the Rising. He was sentenced to execution but reprieved. Some people say that this was because the British placed him at the bottom of an alphabetical list and that by the time his execution was scheduled, further executions were politically unacceptable. Others point to the fact that he had been born in America and believe that the question of US citizenship caused sufficient delay to save his life. In any event, he went on to play a central role in Irish political life: leading the first Dáil; leading the political opposition to the Treaty; founding Fianna Fáil and subsequently heading four governments for a total of twenty-one years. He later served as President of Ireland for two terms.

The Irish Republic emblazoned in gold lettering on a green background provided inspiration to the rebels in the GPO, where the flag flew alongside the tricolour of green, white and orange.

CHAPTER 4

JAMES CONNOLLY'S STATUE

In 1996 a statue commemorating James Connolly was erected opposite Liberty Hall, beside the Custom House. The statue was unveiled by President Mary Robinson. It is interesting to see the wide range of organisations who donated money for this – from the Communist Party of Ireland to that immense corporation and symbol of Irish business, Irish Life plc. The flag that forms the background of the Connolly statue is the 'Starry Plough' or The Plough and the Stars; the plough is the symbol of Labour and the stars represent Socialism. When Connolly came to Dublin, more than half the population was living well below the poverty line. Deaths from tuberculosis were fifty percent higher in Dublin than in any other city of the Empire and infant mortality rates were much higher than in London. Connolly was used to poverty, but was moved by the slum conditions in Dublin and believed he had a strategy for changing them. In 1896 he founded the Irish Socialist Republican Party (ISRP), for the first time connecting the issues of working class and national emancipation.

Up until then, the socialist movement in Ireland had left national issues to one side, concentrating on wages, housing and welfare issues. But Connolly observed that the working class potentially had the most to gain from Irish freedom and were un-corrupted by 'the thousand golden threads' that bound so many Irish businesses to the Empire. Hence the slogan written on the wall behind the statue:

> The cause of Labour is the cause of Ireland and the cause of Ireland is the cause of Labour.

Connolly believed Protestant workers as well as Catholics would benefit from the break with Britain, and tried with some success to create non-sectarian working class organisations in the North.

James Connolly's statue was unveiled on the eightieth anniversary of his execution.

The cry for a 'union of classes' is in reality an insidious move on the part of our Irish master class to have the powers of government transferred from the hands of the English capitalist government into the hands of an Irish capitalist government and to pave the way for this change by inducing the Irish worker to abandon all hopes of bettering his own position.

James Connolly, in the *Workers' Republic*

If Pearse was the poet of the Rising, then Connolly was its main practical organiser. Connolly had carefully studied the street fighting of the Paris Commune of 1871 and the Moscow insurrection of 1906. Connolly, together with Joseph Plunkett, developed the strategy of occupying buildings rather than barricades and of smashing through walls to create interior lines of movement.

The area which is now occupied by the statue was the scene of a huge gathering on that Easter Monday morning in 1916. At 11.30am, the bugler from the Citizen Army, Willie Oman, sounded 'fall-in'. The Volunteers, the ICA, Cumann na mBan and members of Fianna Éireann all formed ranks. They were a motley crew, according

James Connolly was a Scottish Marxist, a writer, an organiser, the Commandant of the Irish Citizen Army, a member of the IRB Military Council and a signatory of the Proclamation. He was wounded in action in the GPO during the Rising, and was tied to a chair and executed in Kilmainham Gaol on 12 May 1916.

to eyewitness accounts, some carrying so many weapons and other material that they would have become very easy targets had the British been able to open fire on them. Most did not have a uniform – in fact only a quarter of the 1,600 men, women and children involved were in fatigues. The majority only had an armband or a green ribbon to indicate which side they were fighting for.

JAMES CONNOLLY

Born of working-class Irish parents in Edinburgh, James Connolly educated himself through his involvement with the socialist movement, becoming a prolific writer. In 1896 Connolly accepted an invitation to come to Ireland as an organiser for a socialist club. He founded the Irish Socialist Republican Party that year, but after a few years of socialist activity in Ireland, Connolly left for America in 1903. During his time in the USA, Connolly was an organiser for the Industrial Workers of the World, a revolutionary syndicalist trade union. In 1910 James Connolly returned to Ireland to join forces with James Larkin in the recently formed Irish Transport and General Workers' Union (ITGWU). With Larkin's departure for America in 1914, Connolly became acting General Secretary of the Union and Commandant of the Irish Citizen Army.

Starting with Seán Heuston's young command, each battalion moved off to their given positions until finally there remained only one group, the GPO column. At the head of this force of about 180 rebels marched Pádraic Pearse with his symbolic swordstick drawn and held high in front of him. Behind Pearse marched James Connolly, some of the onlookers jeering him with the cry: 'there goes Connolly with his pop-guns'. Behind Connolly walked Joseph Plunkett, so ill from an operation the previous week that he had to be held up. He suffered from glandular tuberculosis, and now had a gaping wound in his neck, but was supported by two comrades, on his left Commandant Brennan-Whitmore and on his right an unknown young captain, Michael Collins.

It is a common misconception that all seven members of the

Provisional Government, the seven signatories, were in the General Post Office. In fact, there were five of them in the GPO. The two who were elsewhere were Thomas MacDonagh and Eamonn Ceannt. MacDonagh was in charge of the Second Battalion, commandeering Jacobs' Biscuit Factory, a strong, well-positioned building off George's Street. Eamonn Ceannt led the Fourth Battalion to the South Dublin Union, scene of some of the grimmest fighting in the rebellion [*see* Chapter 1]. Michael Mallin and Countess Markievicz of the Citizen Army were in charge of operations at St Stephen's Green.

WOMEN IN THE RISING

There are two sides to Constance Gore-Booth, or Countess Markievicz as she was usually known: the flamboyant aristocrat and the hard-faced republican socialist. She married a Polish count, but the marriage was not a success. In Stephen's Green on the first day of the Rebellion, she had her women lay out a picnic for the men. A young British soldier was arrested in the park whilst courting his girlfriend; he was told he was now a prisoner of war of the Irish Republic. He asked if he were to be shot, but was informed by his captors that no harm would come to him. He was then taken to the bandstand and issued with cucumber sandwiches and cups of tea. He was overheard to remark that he hoped there would be a Rebellion every day from then on, as the food was 'bloody lovely'.

The other side of the Countess shows that nothing could deter her from her chosen path, and that she had no worries about shooting her large Mauser rifle-pistol. Two rebels informed her that a policeman was refusing to remove himself from the front gates of the park. She ordered her men to shoot him, but as he was a Dubliner they were extremely reluctant to do so. Markievicz went to the gate herself and had no qualms about taking aim alongside two other Volunteers and shooting the constable. Very few people, observing the Countess in polite upper-class society, would have seen the militant determination that lay within her.

Countess Constance Markievicz née Gore-Booth, the aristocratic, bohemian, cofounder of Na Fianna Éireann. An Irish Citizen Army Commandant, she was Lieutenant or Second-in-Command in St Stephen's Green during the Rising.

James Connolly and Countess Markievicz formed a powerful team with mutual respect despite their widely differing backgrounds. They spoke often together on the same public platforms, on both popular and unpopular issues. In 1913, when James Connolly was recovering after a hunger strike against wrongful arrest, he stayed with the Countess at her house in Rathmines.

When it came to the involvement of women in the Rising, there were essentially two traditions present. For many Volunteers, women were there merely to support the military action by providing first aid along with a certain amount of cooking and cleaning. Cumann na mBan was the women's auxiliary to the Volunteers and its members were generally assigned non-military work. Perhaps the most extreme traditionalist was de Valera who refused to have any women under his command, failing to send for Cumann na mBan members who were awaiting orders at Merrion Square. De Valera later said to Hanna Sheehy Skeffington that he regretted his decision, as it meant some of his men had to be assigned cooking duties.

The overall attitude of the Rising was very positive towards women. The wording of the Proclamation is always careful to be inclusive; it begins: 'Irishmen and Irishwomen' and includes the sentence: 'The Irish Republic ... claims the allegiance of every Irishman and Irishwoman.' Given the fact that women had yet to win the vote, this is evidence of a far-sighted sense of equality amongst the rebels.

The most visible sign of a spirit of comradeship between men and women in the Rising was that shown by the Citizen Army. Mallin's force included fifteen women as fighters; indeed the two best snipers in the Stephen's Green force were Markievicz and Margaret Skinnider. Although Markievicz also had links to Cumann na mBan and Na Fianna, she preferred to serve in the Citizen Army precisely because it allowed her to exercise her military skills. As she later said:

> When Connolly began to organise the Irish Citizen Army he brought me along treating me, as he got to know me, as a comrade, giving me any work that I could do and quite ignoring the conventional attitude towards the work of women. This was

his attitude towards women in general; we were never, in his mind, classed for work as a sex, but taken individually and considered, just as every man considers men, and then allotted any work we could do. When he appointed Commandant Mallin as his First Staff Officer, he appointed me as his Second, with the rank of Lieutenant.

The tabloid version of the Easter Rising.

ST STEPHEN'S GREEN

Generally the rebels' military plans and tactics were well thought out, although constantly hampered by smaller numbers than anticipated. But one clear military error occurred when Mallin and Markievicz ordered their men to dig themselves into foxholes and trenches in St Stephen's Green, aping the tactics used in the front lines in France. Newspaper reports of the Great War at the time were expounding the virtues of trench warfare, but however well it may have worked on open land, trench warfare is tactically disastrous when one is surrounded by buildings. Within one day the British were positioned in the Shelbourne Hotel, with a perfect vantage point over the Green.

Michael Mallin, Irish Citizen Army Commandant. He seized St Stephen's Green and the College of Surgeons. Mallin was executed in Kilmainham Gaol on 8 May 1916.

The rebels woke at dawn to the sound and sight of machine-gun bullets raking the soft earth all about them.

The order to evacuate the park was given and the main body escaped into the College of Surgeons, a strong building but lacking strategic importance. There was a constant exchange of sniper fire between the Shelbourne and the College, with an equal number of hits scored by both sides. Mallin was obliged to remove his 'one big union' red hand badge as it was too clear a target. One British soldier mistakenly believed that the rebels would probably not shoot a woman, so he dressed himself in a maid's uniform. However, one of the sharpshooters noticed that a maid with a rather conspicuous beard and moustache was peppering shots in his direction, so he duly returned fire and shot the soldier dead.

St Stephen's Green was the place for another extraordinary story which has become something of a legend. Park-keeper Jim Kearney lived in a cottage in a corner of the park furthest away from the firing. Twice a day he emerged to feed the ducks and twice a day the combatants observed a ceasefire. There is surely an element of black humour shown by such a concern for the welfare of ducks, at a time of far less regard for human life.

CHAPTER 5

LARKIN STATUE, O'CONNELL STREET

The General Post Office, or GPO as it is better known, is in the centre of Dublin's widest boulevard, O'Connell Street. In 1916 this was Sackville Street, but it was renamed after independence to honour the nineteenth-century 'Catholic Emancipator', Daniel O'Connell. The GPO, with its Ionic columns and Athenian style pediment, is an imposing structure, designed by Francis Johnston and opened in 1818. On the roof, three stone figures of Mercury, Hibernia and Fidelity look over the city. At the turn of the century the structure had been undergoing major renovations for twelve years and had reopened in March 1916. In April 1916 the building was to become the headquarters of the Provisional Government.

> We were bitterly disappointed that the fighting had not extended to the country. We swore that, should the fighting ever be resumed, we would be in the thick of it, no matter where it took place.
>
> Dan Breen, *My Fight for Irish Freedom*

Standing proudly upon his plinth beside the GPO is James Larkin, or 'Big Jim' as he is remembered by those who knew him. Larkin was born in Liverpool to Irish parents and became aware of the hardships of life through an accident he suffered while working on the docks. The British-based National Union of Dock Labourers (NUDL) sent Larkin to Ireland to organise Belfast dockers into the union. Larkin was such an accomplished orator that he soon had the city's workers, Catholic and Protestant, united in solidarity and struggling hard against their employers.

Left: A statue of 'Big Jim' Larkin finds its place high upon a plinth in the centre of O'Connell Street.

Below: A world-famous photograph of 'Big Jim' Larkin in characteristic attitude, addressing a huge Labour meeting in Upper O'Connell Street, Dublin, after his return from America in 1923.

The police were sent into the docks to break the strike for the capitalists. Using his impressive speaking skills, Larkin convinced the police that they too were underpaid and a section of the Belfast Metropolitan Police (BMP) went on strike alongside the dockers. However, the more conservative leaders of the NUDL were anxious at the radicalism displayed in Belfast, and 'Big Jim' was suspended from the union. Larkin went to Dublin where, in 1911, he founded his own union based on his belief in militancy and the solidarity strike: the Irish Transport and General Workers' Union.

The significance of Larkin's role in the Easter Rising is that it was from the militancy of the ITGWU that the Irish Citizen Army was formed. As a result of police brutality against workers during the Lockout of 1913, the union formed a volunteer force to patrol their marches and meetings – the Irish Citizen Army.

Larkin himself was in America at the time of the Rising, leaving his colleague and fellow union organiser, James Connolly, in charge of the union and the ICA. Larkin was a believer in the need for Irish independence from Britain, and during the Rising one of the many rumours was that he had returned on a ship with supplies and thousands of Irish-American fighters. Although completely false, because Larkin was in fact facing persecution for his antiwar stance, there was a basis to the rumour: Larkin had indeed spoken about returning on a ship equipped with supplies for disputes, courtesy of the solidarity of US workers.

There is a plaque underneath the statue in three languages giving a quote much repeated by Larkin, but which in all likelihood belongs to Camille Desmoulins (1760–1794), the great French insurrectionary of 1789:

THE GREAT APPEAR GREAT BECAUSE WE ARE ON OUR KNEES – LET US RISE

On the west side of the plinth is a piece by one of Ireland's most popular poets, Patrick Kavanagh, from his poem 'Jim Larkin':

> *And tyranny trampled them in Dublin's gutter*
> *Until Jim Larkin came along and cried*
> *The call of Freedom and the call of Pride*
> *And Slavery crept to its hands and knees*
> *And Nineteen Thirteen cheered from out the utter*
> *Degradation of their miseries.*

On the right-hand side of the statue is a quote from *Drums under the Window* by the playwright Seán O'Casey, author of *The Shadow of a Gunman*, *The Plough and the Stars*, and the famous drama concerning poverty-stricken Dubliners, *Juno and the Paycock*. O'Casey knew Larkin well through the writer's involvement with the Irish Citizen Army. His quote is, therefore, a relevant insight into the character of Larkin:

> He talked to the workers as only Jim Larkin could speak, not for an assignation with peace, dark obedience or placid resignation; but trumpet-tongued of resistance to wrong, discontent with leering poverty, and defiance of any power strutting out to stand in the way of their march onward.

At the crossroads of Sackville Street, Henry Street and Talbot Street there stood Nelson's Pillar. The Pillar was 134 feet tall and Admiral Nelson, the victorious defender, watched over Dublin from this great height. In one sense he was a warning symbol to any revolutionaries who may have hoped for help from the French. 'I have my one good eye on you,' Nelson seemed to say from his plinth. Love him or hate him, Nelson served a dual purpose, as the Pillar was used by Dubliners as a central meeting point.

In 1966 the Irish government planned to have a celebration to commemorate the 1916 Rising. The main parade was to march up O'Connell Street but Nelson, that symbol of British rule, was still on his plinth. The Irish would have been the laughing stock of the

HENRY ST. LOOKING EAST, DUBLIN.

Admiral Nelson's Column, or 'The Pillar' as it was called in Dublin,
was a favourite meeting place but a symbol of British imperialism.

world, celebrating independence underneath their former rulers'
hero, yet at the same time the government could hardly remove
Nelson without causing an international incident with Britain.
Relations between both countries were strained enough as it was,
so speculation has it that the authorities ensured that central
Dublin was particularly quiet in the early hours of the night of 8
March 1966. A few daring republicans climbed the steps of the
Pillar, planted a couple of pounds of explosives underneath
Nelson's statue and blew him sky high. There were no reported
injuries and little damage was done to anything else. The Irish
Army engineers were now legitimately able to consider that the
structure was unsafe and sent in the explosive experts over the
next few days to rig the remainder of the Pillar for detonation.

They ignited their explosives and not only destroyed the column, but every window within half a mile radius.

BRENNAN-WHITMORE'S COMMAND

Across from Nelson's Pillar, at the corner of Talbot Street and Sackville Street [now O'Connell Street], there was a small restaurant called the Pillar Café. Commandant Brennan-Whitmore was given the task of holding this building as part of the defence of the GPO. His first task was to barricade the street by flinging chairs, tables and desks out of the offices that were in the vicinity and using them to build blockades. As he and his comrades were performing their task, he heard a commotion on the street. Looking out of the third-floor window, he saw the 'shawlies', the women of Dublin, running away with his barricade, screaming with joy, 'They're givin' away free furniture!' A countryman himself, Brennan-Whitmore had no experience in dealing with these tough

The destruction of North Earl Street, looking down the street from Nelson's Column.

city women, but as soon as he produced his revolver the women were forced to bring back his barricade.

Brennan-Whitmore remained in communication with the GPO via a metal cord along which a can was pulled containing the messages. One of the Australian soldiers based in Trinity College began a long sniper duel with Brennan-Whitmore's troops, during the course of which he hit the can. This soldier later sought out Brennan-Whitmore in captivity and asked him was the communication interrupted. Brennan-Whitmore replied no, the shooting had hit the can but they could still send messages tied around the wire. Brennan-Whitmore complimented him on his shooting. The Australian soldier merely shrugged, 'I wasn't aiming at the can, but the wire!'

Above and opposite: Two staged photographs showing another use for porter barrels.

The people of the city began to behave in an extraordinary way during the initial few days of the rebellion. There was an atmosphere of excitement and freedom as a result of the lack of a police force and the general mayhem. They began to feel that anarchy was the order of the day and consequently the looting began. Seán O'Casey noted that the first shops these poor people looted were sweet shops and toy shops. There was a certain pathos in the fact that Dublin's most downtrodden could find the nerve to raid tobacconists, but they could not quite bring themselves to attack the obviously more financially rewarding targets such as jewellers' shops. The looters caused stress to the rebels, because their actions could be used to discredit the motives of the uprising. Indeed many British newspapers headlined their stories of the Easter Rising with the word 'Riot'.

All the same, the early buoyant humour of the crowds led to some extraordinary sights. Brennan-Whitmore recounted the tale of a street urchin of about twelve suddenly appearing in golf attire much too large for him:

> Scraping together a little mound of dirt he placed a golf ball upon it with infinite care. The selection of a club seemed to be a weighty affair demanding profound thought. Having at last made up his selection he set himself up in the most approved style and gave several measuring and preliminary swings to his club. Then, driving off, he watched the flight of his ball with hand-shaded eyes; and when finally it came to rest he struck another attitude and exclaimed in peevish tones: 'Bunkered bai Jove!'

In an unfortunate twist to the looting, the people began to set fire to the buildings after they had cleared their contents and this caused additional discomfort to the rebels in the GPO. One building set on fire was a fuel depot for oil lamps, resulting in a fire so intense that the rebels felt its ferocity within the GPO. It is often said that the British destroyed the centre of the city – but the inhabitants also played their part.

CHAPTER 6

INSIDE THE GPO

In the northern doorway of the General Post Office there hangs a stone plaque in two languages. The English text reads:

> Here on Easter Monday 1916, Patrick Pearse read the Proclamation of the Irish Republic. From this building he commanded the forces that asserted in arms Ireland's right to freedom.

This is a direct translation of the Irish text, but underneath there is one solitary line in Irish that has not caught the attention of the translator. The line in English would read:

> It is they who keep the fire alive.

The Irish language has always had a special significance to Republicans, from its revival at the turn of the nineteenth century through to the 1970s when internment was introduced in Northern Ireland – many nationalist prisoners used their time to learn the language of their forefathers. Thomas Davis, the cofounder of *The Nation* newspaper in 1842 and writer of the famous ballad 'A Nation Once Again', said that a nation should guard her language for there is no surer barrier to the march of another nation. When the GPO plaque was erected in the 1960s, there was a revival of nationalist feeling due to the growing crisis in the North. The extra line reflects this.

The Post Office was open for business on that fateful Easter Monday morning when the order was given by James Connolly to charge for the building. The public had by now grown accustomed to the Irish Citizen Army commandeering buildings in mock attacks. This activity had been tolerated by the British, who looked upon Connolly as being more dangerous if persecuted than ignored. Initially the crowd in the GPO was amused by the antics of these 'upstarts', but as soon as the weapons were produced they knew how serious the situation was. One witness wrote:

> A wild scamper was made for the door. Civil servants jumped the counter and ran, some of them not even waiting to procure hat or overcoat.

It so happened that there was a British officer, Lieutenant Chalmers, using the postal facilities at the time. He became the first POW of the rebellion when Captain Michael Collins trussed him up with telephone cable and dumped him in a telephone

Citizens and carters going about their daily business in front of the GPO after the Rising.

Left: A British soldier stands guard over the ruined GPO after the Rising.

booth. Later on in the week a surgeon, Captain Mahony from the Indian Medical Corps, was arrested at a rebel barricade and brought to the GPO only hours after arriving in Dublin from India. Mahony is chiefly remembered for the fact that he volunteered to serve in the temporary hospital that had been erected in the post office, feeling that he was a doctor first and a British soldier second. Those who served in the GPO remember him as a gentleman, who never used his new position to try to escape or distract the rebels from their objectives.

While upstairs rebel telegraphists amused themselves with the growing number of queries on the wires, the troops in the main hall undertook preparations for conflict. All the glass in the tall front windows of the building was smashed to prevent injury from flying shards during any potential exchanges of gunfire. The Volunteers then commandeered the thousands of leather-bound ledgers and journals within which every stamp that had been bought or sold was recorded. They placed the books like breeze-blocks on top of the window sills, ensuring that these extremely effective barricades were loopholed. The loopholes enabled the snipers to peep or shoot at any target that would appear within their range.

A workman climbs a ladder (right), perhaps beginning the long task of reconstructing the inside of the GPO.

THE LANCERS' CHARGE

The garrison expected many full frontal assaults on their position, knowing that it would not be long before the British discovered that the GPO was the rebel HQ. The first and, as it transpired, only full frontal assault on the GPO occurred at 3pm, only hours into the Rising. News of the impending attack reached the rebels when the crowd of onlookers on Sackville Street scattered towards O'Connell Bridge, shouting at the garrison that they were 'for it now'. A regiment of the hated British Lancers, with their shiny brass and leather uniforms, came trotting down Sackville Street to see what all the commotion was about. All the rebels trained their sights on the unsuspecting soldiers. James Connolly ordered that no one was to shoot until the Lancers had passed in front of the rebel position.

Fortune was shining upon the Lancers that hour. One of the Kimmage men, standing on top of the roof of the GPO, ignited his home-made bomb with the intention of flinging it amongst the troops. The bomb exploded prematurely and seriously injured him. With the sound of the explosion and the Kimmage man's cries of pain, the rebels began to fire wildly at the Lancers, who were still a little too far away to suffer serious casualties. One of them was killed outright and a couple of others were wounded, but it was not the massacre that it could have been.

One of the horses fell to his death just outside the GPO. The horse became a major environmental problem for the occupiers, who were sickened by the smell of the rotting corpse. The weather at the time was unseasonably hot; there were five days of pure sunshine during that Easter week, and if one has ever encountered an Irish April, one can understand why some of the rebels took it as a sign from God that He approved of their actions. Elder citizens of this state still refer to a few days of sunshine as 'Rebellion Weather'.

The main significance of this short encounter was that the British turned on their heels and, for the first time in Ireland since 1798, were seen to retreat from the fight. The rebels were elated. Even those leaders of the Rising who considered the venture a blood sacrifice began to wonder if military success might be achievable. Perhaps a small insurrectionary army would be quite capable of defeating such a 'cowardly force'. It later transpired that the Lancers judged that there must have been thousands of insurgents within the confines of the GPO and thus decided to return to base to report this situation.

TUNNELLING IN THE GPO

Meanwhile, tunnelling began in the Republican HQ. Holes were knocked through adjoining walls from the GPO all the way down the street to the quays of the Liffey. This served a few purposes, the main one being to achieve undetectable movement over a large area, particularly in order to check on the movements of British soldiers along the quays. As the Metropole Hotel was adjacent to the Post Office, it was also hoped that food for the men could be brought through the tunnels. One rebel sent a sample from a flour-sack to the hastily assembled GPO food preparation area, but it was found to contain only sawdust.

When Citizen Army men entered the Imperial Hotel, owned by William Martin Murphy, they avenged themselves on his conduct during the 1913 Lockout by flying their flag, the Starry Plough, from the building. This had the consequence of ensuring its destruction – at the hands of British artillery.

The interior of the Imperial Hotel, a fine establishment which once graced Sackville Street (now O'Connell Street), opposite the GPO. The hotel was destroyed by fire during the Rising.

From his arrival at 4am on the Tuesday, and his assumption of command, General Lowe decided not to attack the GPO due to the intelligence of the Lancers that there were too many rebels there. Instead he planned to contain the rebellion within the confine of the two canals which circle Dublin, the Grand Canal on the south side and the Royal Canal on the north side. Lowe also ordered that interlinking cordons of British troops were to surround rebel strongholds and strangle the insurgents into submission. This cautious, although ultimately effective, tactic of strangulation had an unexpected effect upon the garrison of the GPO: boredom. After the adrenaline-filled moments of the opening encounter, a long lull fell over the rebel HQ. Men and women were tense with expectation of battle, but none came.

A couple of Citizen Army men approached James Connolly and requested permission to go home. When Connolly asked them if they were scared they indignantly replied in the negative, but said that they had to go to work the next morning. Their leader smiled and let them know that there would be 'no work tomorrow or the next day'.

To quell the restlessness of the troops, over the next two days Pearse began to issue manifestos and a newspaper was written from within the GPO. There were cheers when the rebels read that Jim Larkin had arrived in Mayo with fifty thousand Irish-Americans to come to their aid, and that the whole country had risen in defiance of MacNeill's countermanding order. The publications also stated, this time truthfully, that the young commander Seán Heuston and his boys were holding out under intense pressure at the Mendicity Institution.

A young Cockney socialist from the Citizen Army, John Neale, was found to be taking pot shots at Nelson's nose from the roof of the GPO. It took a sharp order from Connolly to stop this needless waste of ammunition. This young man lost his life later on in the week when another rebel stumbled and dropped his shotgun, which misfired against an ammunition belt, sending bullets in all directions. One of them lodged in Neale's gut. Asked if he was badly hurt he replied, 'I'm dying, Comrade,' and lay down amongst some mailbags. If one takes a close look at Nelson's head, which is in the Dublin Civic Museum, one can clearly discern a bullet wound to the right of the nose.

The Provisional Government
... TO THE ...
CITIZENS OF DUBLIN

The Provisional Government of the Irish Republic salutes the CITIZENS OF DUBLIN on the momentous occasion of the proclamation of a

Sovereign Independent Irish State

now in course of being established by Irishmen in Arms.

The Republican forces hold the lines taken up at Twelve noon on Easter Monday, and nowhere, despite fierce and almost continuous attacks of the British troops, have the lines been broken through. The country is rising in answer to Dublin's call, and the final achievement of Ireland's freedom is now, with God's help, only a matter of days. The valour, self sacrifice, and discipline of Irish men and women are about to win for our country a glorious place among the nations.

Ireland's honour has already been redeemed ; it remains to vindicate her wisdom and her self-control.

All citizens of Dublin who believe in the right of their Country to be free will give their allegiance and their loyal help to the Irish Republic. There is work for everyone: for the men in the fighting line, and for the women in the provision of food and first aid. Every Irishman and Irishwoman worthy of the name will come forward to help their common country in this her supreme hour.

Able-bodied Citizens can help by building barricades in the streets to oppose the advance of the British troops. The British troops have been firing on our women and on our Red Cross. On the other hand, Irish Regiments in the British Army have refused to act against their fellow countrymen.

The Provisional Government hopes that its supporters — which means the vast bulk of the people of Dublin — will preserve order and self-restraint. Such looting as has already occurred has been done by hangers-on of the British Army. Ireland must keep her new honour unsmirched.

We have lived to see an Irish Republic proclaimed. May we live to establish it firmly, and may our children and our children's children enjoy the happiness and prosperity which freedom will bring.

Signed on behalf of the Provisional Government,

P. H. PEARSE,

Commanding in Chief the Forces of the Irish Republic, and President of the Provisional Government.

Pádraic Pearse read out this manifesto to a large crowd of onlookers at Nelson's Column on Tuesday evening during Easter Week 1916.

THE GUNS BEGIN

By Wednesday of Easter Week the situation in the Post Office began to alter radically. Contrary to Connolly's conviction that a capitalist government would never destroy property by shelling

The Metropole, a five star hotel, stands in ruins beside the GPO and Nelson's Column.

their positions, the British began to utilise two nine-pounder guns brought up from Athlone. These were installed, with the help of British sympathisers, at the corner of D'Olier Street and West-moreland Street, in order to bombard the rebels out of their position. Incendiary devices and explosives pounded the Metropole Hotel, next door to the GPO. The first shells actually destroyed the offices of the *Freeman's Journal*, a paper that supported Redmond and his National Volunteers; this hit brought forth a chorus of approval from the rebels. Then the shells began to rain down upon the roof of the GPO. Initially the men were able to deal with the incendiaries with buckets of sand and water hoses. But soon the firing from the big guns of the *Helga* gunboat also began to batter at the rebel position. One survivor wrote:

> The heat from the burning block opposite the GPO was beyond belief. Despite the great width of O'Connell Street, the sacks and binders in the windows began to scorch, showing signs of smouldering. Batches of men had to be hastily formed to continually drench the window fortifications with water.

So hot indeed was it that this water would turn to steam on coming into contact with the smouldering ledgers.

The shelled remains of the offices of the *Freeman's Journal,* ironically a Redmonite newspaper that supported volunteering for the British Army.

CONNOLLY WOUNDED

Earlier, Commandant Connolly issued an order concerning new positions along Henry Street. He came out of the GPO and pointed out the various places to be occupied, but upon his return sniper fire was pouring down the street. A bullet from a British sniper wounded him in the shoulder. Re-entering the GPO, Connolly went quietly to the young volunteer McLoughlin, a medical student who had been training for more than ten years. After treatment by Dr Mahony, Connolly asked that no one else be informed of his injury and tried to hide it beneath his jacket.

Later on, during the bombardment of Sackville Street, Connolly chose thirty men to occupy the *Irish Independent* newspaper offices with the purpose of stopping a British charge down Middle Abbey Street. The Commandant was watching the progress of his men from a back lane, happy that he had chosen John MacLoughlin, a sixteen-year-old, to lead the party of Volunteers. MacLoughlin had already earned a reputation for himself as a clear thinker and a brave fighter. He had been taking messages between the Mendicity Institution, the Four Courts and the GPO – so he had learned the hard way where British positions were and had dodged many a sniper's bullet. Unfortunately, Connolly was a little less cautious and suddenly a ricochet bullet drove into the Commandant's ankle, shattering the bone and inflicting a potentially lethal wound. Now alone, Connolly had to crawl an agonising distance until he reached the relative safety of the GPO. He was

Walter Paget's impression of the scene inside the GPO during the Rising. Connolly lies wounded on the stretcher surrounded by his fellow rebel leaders and comrades. It is worth noting that many survivors from the GPO applauded this water-colour for its faithful rendition of the scene.

tended to immediately by Mahony, who saw that the leg was irreparable. Despite his judgement that Connolly must be in tremendous pain, the surgeon could only administer a weak painkiller and attach a crude splint to his ankle.

Although Connolly spent the remaining time of the occupation lying on a stretcher, he continued to issue orders. His determination and strength made a great impression on Pearse, who wrote in one of his missives:

> If I were to mention names of individuals, my list would be a long one. I will name only that of Commandant-General James Connolly, Commanding the Dublin Division. He lies wounded, but is still the guiding brain of our resistance.

GPO ABANDONED

The situation in the GPO was becoming more and more desperate and the men needed every encouragement they could get. Due to the intensity of the bombardment the roof of the building was collapsing in sections. The extreme heat from the raging fires that were engulfing half the street was causing considerable discomfort to the rebels. Slates and molten tar were falling constantly from above and the ground was covered in inches of water from the fire hoses, which were now so riddled with bullet holes that they were practically useless.

A most notable act was the rescue of a wounded man by George Plunkett. He heard a man crying in pain on the other side of the barricades. Risking life and limb, he climbed over amid a fresh hail of machine-gun fire and hauled the man to safety. It is well documented that he was not even slightly disappointed to discover that he had nearly been killed saving a young British squaddie. In fact, when he did discover that it was an enemy soldier he returned to the spot to fetch his rifle.

By Friday the rebels realised the hopelessness of their position. Before the whole building became engulfed in flames, Pearse gave the order for the women to evacuate. The women Volunteers insisted that as they had been there from the beginning they would stay until the end, and after a meeting with Pearse they forced him to retract his order. Winifred Carney was Connolly's loyal secretary and was devoted to him. A socialist, she disliked Plunkett for his aristocratic bearing, although her opinion of him changed when he gave her a ring from his finger for his sweetheart, Grace Gifford, Thomas MacDonagh's sister in law. Plunkett felt he would never see Grace again and this act touched Miss Carney, who knew that the two were engaged to be married.

Louise Gavan Duffy was Chief Assistant to Quartermaster Desmond FitzGerald and had also found time to feed the garrison, along with Peggy Downey and Mae Murray. All three had been the first to complain when it was suggested that they should evacuate. Elizabeth O'Farrell and Julia Grenan from Cumann na mBan, two caring nurses who tended to the wounded even as the bombardment of the GPO was at its height, also stayed on.

Finally, the order for the GPO battalion to abandon their position was given. It was decided that an initial charge should be made down Henry Street by a dozen men to secure Williams and Woods, a large factory on Great Britain Street, and to make this the new garrison HQ. The O'Rahilly volunteered to lead this dangerous expedition. It was The O'Rahilly who had driven around the country with Eoin MacNeill's countermanding order, and who had been so annoyed that the IRB had kidnapped Bulmer Hobson before the rebellion that he went to Pearse brandishing a revolver, threatening to shoot the first person who tried the same tactics on him. Yet he joined in the rebellion when he realised it was going ahead despite the attempts he and MacNeill had made to stop it. Many years later Yeats wrote a ballad, 'The O'Rahilly', which indicated his stance:

> *'Am I such a craven that*
> *I should not get the word*
> *But for what some travelling man*

Had heard I had not heard?'
Then on Pearse and Connolly
He fixed a bitter look,
'Because I helped to wind the clock
I come to hear it strike.'

Michael Joseph O'Rahilly, otherwise
known simply as 'The O'Rahilly', Kerry
journalist, Director of Arms for the Irish
Volunteers, he brought MacNeill's
countermanding order to the southwest
but fought from the GPO during the
Rising. 'The O'Rahilly' was killed leading
a charge down Moore Street as part of
the evacuation of the GPO.

Unfortunately for The O'Rahilly and the twelve men who made
the charge down Henry Street, only four of them survived it un-
harmed. A machine-gun, manned by Sherwood Foresters, was
waiting for them at a British barricade at the intersection of Great
Britain Street and Moore Street. Riddled by bullet holes, The
O'Rahilly died slowly. Four hours after he was shot he was heard
asking for water. A further nineteen hours passed, as had the moment of surrender, when a military ambulance came across him,
still barely alive. The officer in charge of the vehicle was heard to
reply to a query:

> That's a Sinn Féin officer – the more of them that die naturally,
> the fewer we'll have to shoot.

On The O'Rahilly's body was found a poignant message to his
wife:

> Written after I was shot ... I was hit leading a rush ... I got more
> than one bullet I think ... It was a good fight anyhow.

As Pearse and Mac Diarmada were giving instructions to everyone on how to get to Williams and Woods, John MacLoughlin
(freshly returned from the *Irish Independent* offices) intervened,
announcing that this factory and, in fact, most of Great Britain
Street were in the hands of the British. It dawned on the rebels
that The O'Rahilly was on his way to a suicidal position and, before any decision was made regarding a line of retreat, a disorganised charge down Henry Street took place in order to assist him.

The Dublin Bread Company and bombarded buildings on Lower Sackville Street.

The British machine-guns went into overdrive, raking the
streets as the rebels poured out of the GPO and scattering the
men in all directions. There was mass confusion and no officer
seemed to be in charge until MacLoughlin began to take it upon

himself to issue orders specifically to build a barricade out of any available materials. Volunteers were scattering everywhere amid the general mayhem, some going into a warehouse on Henry Street, others breaking into houses, and others too frightened to move. Eventually a building was chosen by MacLoughlin, Mac Diarmada, Clarke and Plunkett, the leaders assisting the Volunteers to barricade it. Now it became a little quieter, the machine-guns dying with the light of day.

Pearse was one of the last to leave the burning GPO, like the captain going down with his ship. With Willie, his faithful brother, and a couple of Volunteers he made his way to the new temporary headquarters of the Provisional Irish Government. This was, symbolically, a modest grocer's shop, Coogan's, on the corner of Henry Place and Moore Street – a far cry from the imposing and elaborately decorated General Post Office.

Willie Pearse was Pádraic Pearse's younger brother. A Private in the Irish Volunteers, he was stationed in the GPO during the Rising and executed in Kilmainham Gaol on 4 May 1916.

CHAPTER 7

THE HA'PENNY BRIDGE

From the Ha'penny Bridge the view upstream of the Liffey to the copper dome of the Four Courts is very clear. Commandant Ned Daly was there, in charge of the Volunteers' First Battalion and had, it may be remembered, discovered the police hidden in their own cells in Bridewell Station, near the Four Courts.

The Four Courts garrison's command of Grattan Bridge was a serious impediment to the British forces' ability to move across Dublin. This position also provided protection for those rebels from County Dublin who were gradually filtering into the city via the quays on the north side of the river. Thus it was a great breakthrough for the British when an enterprising officer managed to think of a method for crossing the bridge and bringing artillery to attack the garrison in the Four Courts.

> You have reached your doom,
> Your hour is come.
> My sword will flash,
> And not softly.
>
> Cúchulainn to Ferdia, from *Táin Bó Cuailnge*
> (set down *c*. AD 750)

He approached Guinness's brewery, across the river from the Four Courts, and commandeered two huge boilers. The boilers were taken via truck to the railway engineering works, where they were fashioned into armoured cars. Rifle holes were drilled through the thick metal plate and false holes painted on the outside to distract fire. The improvised armoured cars proved extremely useful and by Thursday the Four Courts was heavily besieged, as under protection of the vehicles soldiers could safely cross the bridge and gain control of the quays.

The east wing of the Four Courts, commanded by Edward Daly, with bullet holes just visible.

After this success, an armoured car was brought up to Sackville Street. However, here the story took a different turn when an accurate piece of sniping killed the driver of the strange machine. One can only imagine the unpleasant experience of the eighteen British troops inside the vehicle, trapped throughout a long day, sun beating down on the former vat. Guinness may generally have a welcoming smell, but when you are immobile, waiting for darkness and hoping a bullet will not find its way inside the vehicle, you are liable to be put off the drink for life.

Up until then the British strategy of containing the Rising by

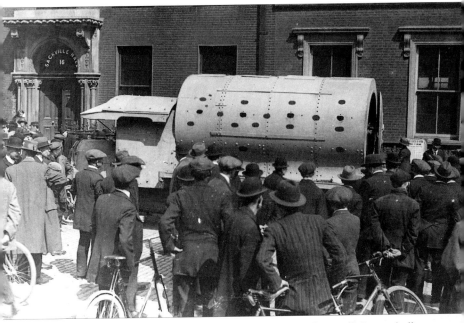

A hastily assembled armoured personnel vehicle made from a Guinness boiler.

encircling it had not been fully implemented. A gap existed in their cordon, as they had mistaken the rebel positions to the north of the Four Courts. The GPO garrison is estimated to have doubled from the arrival of reinforcements throughout the Rising. As General Maxwell later explained:

> One line of the cordon was to pass through North King Street. We discovered, however, that instead of being outside the rebel area the street actually cut through it, and very desperate fighting occurred before we could complete the cordon in this street.

The 'desperate fighting' that Maxwell refers to is not an exaggeration. The close proximity of troops inside and around buildings led to a murderously intimate confrontation mainly centred around 'Reilly's Fort', a pub in front of which a republican flag had been planted on a captured lance.

The flames from burning buildings became so bright on the

Thursday of the Rising that one Volunteer claimed that 'a pin could be picked up by the glare overspreading the surrounding streets.' However, the severest fighting took place in pitch darkness along deserted streets and was conducted by boring through the walls of houses, firing at flashes, with a scream or groan to indicate a hit. Occasionally the British forces lit up the sky with strange tints from their star shells.

Sackville Street in flames during the Rising. Some rebels feared they would be burnt alive in the GPO.

NORTH KING STREET

One important consequence of the bitter fighting in this area was that a group of British soldiers apparently lost control and, as they battered their way into houses along North King Street, killed residents indiscriminately. The discovery of a shallow grave after the Rising that contained two civilian bodies later led to an investigation, which served to help the decisive shift of public opinion against the British forces.

The Ha'penny Bridge leads to Temple Bar, which is now a tourist friendly part of Dublin. The whole area retains its cobbled roadways, a reminder of how the streets would have appeared in 1916. During the Rising, the rebels scattered glass on the major junctions to frustrate the movement of cavalry. If you look carefully between the cobbles there is plenty of glass to be seen worn smooth now between the stones – although it would take extraordinary expertise to pick out 1916 glass from more recent additions of a non-military nature!

NEWS AND RUMOURS

On the Tuesday of the Rising, Augustine Birrell, the Chief Secretary for Ireland, issued the following press statement:

> At noon yesterday serious disturbances broke out in Dublin. A large body of men identified with the Sinn Féiners, mostly armed, occupied Stephen's Green, and took possession forcibly of the Post Office, where they cut the telegraph and telephone wires. Houses were occupied in Stephen's Green, Sackville Street, Abbey Street, and along the quays.
>
> In the course of the day soldiers arrived from the Curragh, and the situation is now well in hand ...

This statement was faithfully reproduced by the country's leading newspapers. The Rising was doubly marginalised by *The Irish Times,* which devoted the major part of its front page to the Fairyhouse races. The rebellion only featured in a short article at the bottom of the page, taken almost entirely from Birrell.

However, this was the last that any newspaper was to say about the Rising for some time. *The Irish Times* and the *Irish Independent* buildings were taken over by rebels from the GPO. The *Express* building on the other side of Dame Street, at City Hall, was occupied by fighters under the command of Seán Connolly. The only publication to reach the eyes of Dubliners during the Rising was the small four-page newsheet, *Irish War News*, put out by the rebels themselves from the Post Office.

Given the absence of information, and the intense desire to find out about events, Dublin crowds gathered and passed on news by word of mouth. Some of the rumours were surprisingly accurate, in particular regarding the rebel positions. But, of course, all sorts of extraordinary stories began to circulate. James Stephens, that wonderful observer of the range of human behaviour, saw the process by which wild stories were spread:

> Earlier in the day I met a wild individual who spat rumour as though his mouth were a machine gun or a linotype machine. He believed everything he heard; and everything he heard became as by magic favourable to his hopes, which were violently anti-English. One unfavourable rumour was instantly crushed by him with three stories which were favourable and triumphantly so ...
>
> I think this man created and winged every rumour that flew in Dublin, and he was the sole individual whom I heard definitely taking a side. He left me, and, looking back, I saw him pouring his news into the ear of a gaping stranger whom he had arrested for the purpose. I almost went back to hear would he tell the same tale or would he elaborate it into a new thing, for I am interested in the art of storytelling.

MACBRIDE

As John MacBride walked down Dame Street on the first day of the rebellion, he came across a marching band of rebels. At the lead walked Thomas MacDonagh, on his way to take over Jacobs' Biscuit Factory. MacBride hailed MacDonagh and was informed that the rebellion was to go ahead despite the countermanding order. Because MacBride had military experience, having fought against the British in South Africa, MacDonagh gave this veteran Volunteer the second highest rank in the Jacobs' garrison. As the fighting went on throughout the week, MacBride wanted to 'fight them like the Boers', instead of waiting for the British to attack their positions.

MacBride had been married to Maud Gonne, reputedly the most beautiful woman in Ireland. The marriage ended in divorce, much to the excitement of the poet William Butler Yeats. Yeats's love poetry reflects his unrequited love for Maud Gonne, who was

Thomas MacDonagh was a teacher and professor of English, a poet, a Gaelic League enthusiast, Director of Training for the Irish Volunteers, an IRB Military Council member and signatory of the Proclamation. During the Rising he acted as Commandant of the garrison stationed at Jacobs' Biscuit Factory. MacDonagh was executed in Kilmainham Gaol on 3 May 1916.

a founding member of *Inginidhe Na hÉireann* (Daughters of Ireland), a women's group dedicated to Irish independence and the promotion of Irish culture. The poem 'Easter 1916' reflects Yeats's feeling for John MacBride:

> *This other man I had dreamed*
> *A drunken, vainglorious lout.*
> *He had done most bitter wrong*
> *To some who are near my heart . . .*

MacBride was executed for his part in the Rising; the British were pleased to be rid of the Major, who had been a thorn in their side for so long. Yet his role in the rebellion was rather accidental. It is likely that the reason the British assumed

MacBride was a senior figure amongst republicans was the prominent role played by Maud Gonne in the national movement. John MacBride was survived by his son, Seán, who went on to move from Chief of Staff of the IRA to the head of Clann na Poblachta, a radical republican political party which formed part of a coalition government in 1948.

LITERARY CONNECTIONS

Another son of a rebel who went on to great fame was Donagh MacDonagh, son of Thomas, the third signatory of the Proclamation. His father was a poet and MacDonagh carried on the tradition to become a well-respected scribe himself. One of his better-known poems is 'Dublin Made Me'. He may well have taken inspiration for his way of life from the poem his father wrote for him, 'Wishes for my Son':

> *Now, my son, is life for you,*
> *And I wish you joy of it, –*
> *Joy of power in all you do,*
> *Deeper passion, better wit*
> *Than I had who had enough,*
> *Quicker life and length thereof,*
> *More of every gift but love.*

There are some great connections between the literary characters of the time and the rebels. The Anglo-Irish literary revival is often credited with being one of the catalysts for the rebellion, but one wonders if Yeats overemphasised his part when he wrote:

> *Did that play of mine send out, certain men the English shot?*

The fact is that Pearse's own writings and poetry show a man dedicated to freeing his country through revolution, as can be seen in his poem 'The Rebel':

And I say to my people's masters: Beware,
Beware of the thing that is coming, beware of the risen people,
Who shall take what ye would not give. Did ye think to conquer
    the people,
Or that Law is stronger than life and than men's desire to be free?

Joseph Mary Plunkett, the seventh signatory, was also a poet and a scholar. His poem, 'This Heritage to the Race of Kings', is a powerful call for a new generation to take up the struggle for Irish freedom:

This heritage to the race of kings –
Their children and their children's seed
Have wrought their prophecies in deed
Of terrible and splendid things.

The hands that fought, the hearts that broke
In old immortal tragedies,
These have not failed beneath the skies,
Their children's heads refuse the yoke.

And still their hands shall guard the sod
That holds their father's funeral urn,
Still shall their hearts volcanic burn
With anger of the sons of God.

No alien sword shall earn as wage
The entail of their blood and tears,
No shameful price for peaceful years
Shall ever part this heritage.

Plunkett had the benefit of close ties with the literary world and was a personal friend of Thomas MacDonagh, working with him as

Director of the Irish Theatre and editing the *Irish Review*. Erskine Childers, author of *The Riddle of the Sands,* is a typical example of one of the characters that MacDonagh fraternised with. It was Childers' yacht, the *Asgard,* that landed the Volunteers' arms shipment at Howth in 1914.

James Connolly, although not a literary figure, taught himself to write and edit a newspaper, developing a dry satirical style which, together with his sharp political insight, made his writings very memorable. His works are still published and much read. Connolly also turned his hand to Labour songs – such as 'A Rebel Song':

> *Come workers sing a rebel song*
> *A song of love and hate*
> *Of love unto the lowly*
> *And of hatred to the great.*
> *The great who trod our fathers down,*
> *Who steal our children's bread,*
> *Whose hands of greed are stretched to rob*
> *The living and the dead.*

At the time of the Easter Rising the writings of those involved would have been known only to a relatively small audience. But after their deaths a tremendous interest in their work grew up. As the poems, writings and songs of the rebels were reprinted and read, they helped to convince large numbers of people that the organisers of the Rising were not crude militaristic criminals, as portrayed in the press, but rather an educated and thoughtful body of people acting out of a deep sense of principle.

CHAPTER 8

THE ENTRANCE TO DUBLIN CASTLE

Dublin Castle in 1916 was the centuries-old centre of governance of Ireland. On the Easter Monday, the Castle not only contained all its usual files and documents, but three of the most senior members of the British administration. In a twist of fate Sir Matthew Nathan, His Majesty's Under Secretary for Ireland, had invited Major Ivor Price, the Military Intelligence Officer, and A.H. Norway as Secretary of the Post Office, to his office to discuss the proposed arrests of 'Sinn Féiners'. Their meeting had been planned for 12 noon, so they had only sat down to talk when the Castle was attacked by the very men whom they wished to lock up. The usual heavy garrison was absent. The Chief Secretary for Ireland, Augustine Birrell, having learned of the capture of Roger Casement and having read the Volunteers' Chief of Staff Eoin MacNeill's countermanding order in the papers the previous day, saw no reason to cancel the leave that troops had been given in order to enjoy the fine weather and an eagerly awaited bank holiday trip to the Fairyhouse races.

An anonymous British writer, who was in the Castle at the time, wrote later of the Rising that:

Even the best informed in the place, I think, regarded such a happening as a very remote possibility.

In the event only two officers (a colonel and a major) were present, along with wounded and disabled soldiers and some policemen.

The weakness of the Castle's defences presented the rebels with the possibility of an extraordinary coup: three invaluable hostages and all the information at the disposal of the British administration. No newspaper report could marginalise a Rising that had seized Dublin Castle. However, when Captain Seán Connolly (no relation to James) brought his Citizen Army troops to the Castle entrance, they restricted themselves to capturing the guardroom before moving to the nearby City Hall.

This missed opportunity has sometimes been used as criticism of Seán Connolly. However, the poor turnout for the rebellion meant that Connolly's initial forces consisted of only twenty-five fighters. Since the Castle was expected to hold several hundred British troops, his decision to occupy City Hall seems eminently sensible – from its high copper-domed roof the Castle garrison could be pinned down. The rebels were well prepared for the seizure of City Hall, having had keys to the building made up in advance.

Connolly sent some of his small force to the *Express* offices across Dame Street, and their line of fire proved particularly dangerous to the British. The same British witness remembered that:

> One of the worst points, so far as we were concerned, was the newspaper office just facing the Castle gates, which seemed to have a very strong garrison of Sinn Féiners, including some amazingly good marksmen.

The British too had their own sharpshooters, and Seán Connolly's command ended abruptly on the rooftops as he was shot in the head by a sniper, becoming one the first casualties of the Rising.

A bomb had destroyed the phone lines between Dublin Castle and the British Army GHQ. But the occupants of the Castle were fortunate in that the line to the Crown Alley telephone exchange remained in use. Nor did the rebel commanders see fit to occupy this exchange, which lay within the area under their control in Temple Bar. As soon as British reinforcements were available, they were brought to the Castle – experiencing some difficulty in finding a safe route from the station. By nightfall the balance of forces had turned irreversibly.

During the night the British troops managed to break into the ground floor of City Hall. In the darkness and confusion there was a certain amount of fighting between different units of the British Army. A woman was discovered, Jenny Shanahan, who quick-wittedly thanked her deliverers. She was brought under the protection of a gallant officer, who looked after her courteously in the hope of information concerning the strength of the rebel force. This Jenny was quite prepared to divulge, saying that there must be hundreds of the Citizen Army upstairs. The British soldiers promptly called off their attack and retreated from the building until dawn. This must have delighted Jenny Shanahan, for she was of course a rebel – mistaken for a civilian due to her lack of a uniform. Unfortunately, Jenny's friends were not so quick-witted, and when, later, she was made to visit the cells in order to identify leaders, they cried out in relief at finding Jenny alive – only to ensure that she joined them in prison.

SURRENDER

We left the leaders of the rebellion as they retreated from the GPO across to the shops and houses around Henry Street. Mrs Coogan, the proprietor of the shop that was now occupied by five signatories of the Proclamation, saw a dying Connolly and a hungry crowd of Volunteers. She gave them a shoulder of boiled ham, an act of kindness the rebel leaders gratefully acknowledged. It was then decided that young John MacLoughlin should be given Connolly's rank and he was thus made a commandant. It was also decided that tunnels should be dug through the walls of the block of houses to Hanlon's fishmongers at number 16, Moore Street, which was to become the final rebel HQ at dawn on Saturday morning.

As the morning became brighter the commanders gathered their thoughts on what should be their next move. They were surrounded on all sides by British troops but MacLoughlin, knowing the lie of the land, reckoned it would be tactically better to charge

Top: Citizens view the remains of Henry Street.

Below: Abbey Street suffered extensive damage from the British bombardment of the city centre. The Royal Hibernian Academy was ruined and many great works of art were lost forever.

towards the Four Courts, meet up with Ned Daly and his men and then perhaps fight towards the mountains. Without a doubt this was the most logical plan, as they would have been burned out eventually and met their deaths like trapped animals. The plan was ratified by all and MacLoughlin set out to search for volunteers to lead an advance party. While he was away, Pearse witnessed an incident that was to have a profound effect upon the Commandant-General. The Flag pub had caught fire and its owner, Robert Dillon, his wife and his daughter came out of the building waving the inevitable white flag. They were mown down by an over-enthusiastic British machine-gunner. Pearse probably felt a certain amount of guilt; after all, the blood sacrifice was to be

Edward Daly, Commandant of the Four Courts area during the Rising. He was executed at dawn on 4 May 1916.

self-sacrifice and should not have included young girls. He knew that more citizens and rebels would lose their lives if a breakthrough was attempted. Upon consultation with the rest of the leaders, Pearse asked Nurse Elizabeth O'Farrell to go and let the British know that terms should be agreed. They would surrender.

Elizabeth O'Farrell, waving her white flag, safely reached the British barricade whereupon an officer led her to Tom Clarke's tobacconist shop, scene of many a secret IRB meeting. O'Farrell announced that the Commandant of the Irish Republican Army was ready to speak with the Commandant of the British Army. General Lowe, in Trinity College, as opposed to the latest arrival on the scene, General Maxwell, jumped in his staff car and was driven to meet the nurse. Lowe informed O'Farrell that she must

An emotional moment for the President of the Provisional Government, Pádraic Pearse, surrendering to General Lowe on Saturday afternoon, 29 April 1916.

tell Pearse that no conditions for surrender could be met – Pearse had naively hoped that the British would take him and allow the rest of the rebels to go free. Returning to Pearse with the message from the British General, Nurse O'Farrell agreed to bring Pearse to meet Lowe at the top of Moore Street. The two commanders met for the first time; Pearse handed Lowe his sword, a photographer snapped the occasion and Pearse was whisked off to appear before General Maxwell.

At Parkgate in Kilmainham, Maxwell insisted that Pearse sign several surrender notes. The full text of these is as follows:

In order to prevent the further slaughter of Dublin citizens, and in the hope of saving the lives of our followers now surrounded and hopelessly outnumbered, the members of the Provisional Government present at Headquarters have agreed to an unconditional surrender, and the Commandants of the various districts in the City and Country will order their commands to lay down arms.

PH Pearse, 29 April 1916, 3.45pm

James Connolly added beneath the typewritten note a further scrawled sentence:

> I agree to these conditions for the men only under my own command in the Moore Street District and for the men in the Stephen's Green Command.

This was to cover the Citizen Army members, who would not otherwise necessarily accept the surrender order from Pearse alone.

Rebels under arrest being marched to prison. Most insurrectionists were eventually sent to English or Welsh detention centres, serving as a reminder of the deportations suffered by previous generations of Irish rebels.

That night, Elizabeth O'Farrell found herself in a room whose window overlooked a small field in the grounds of the Rotunda Hospital on Parnell Square. She was outraged that despite the prisoner of war status of the rebels, they were herded into the field and forced to spend the night in the cold with no amenities. When the surrendered rebels stood up, stiff-legged, at 9am on Sunday morning, a cloud of steam rose with them.

During the course of the night the prisoners had been subjected to insults and an occasional punch. Matters had deteriorated in the early morning with the arrival of Captain Lee Wilson to take charge of the British ring of bayonets. Wilson rushed about in fits of anger, abusing the rebels and seizing personal possessions – including Mac Diarmada's walking stick. Wilson was to pay a price for this display. In January 1920, during the War of Independence, he was shot in Gorey, County Wexford, where he was District Inspector of the Royal Irish Constabulary (RIC).

Irish Rebellion – May 1916.
Soldiers bivouacking opposite Liberty Hall
the Rebel Headquarters in Dublin.

British soldiers after the successful capture and bombardment of the somewhat empty Liberty Hall.

To the victor the spoils of war. British officers show off the captured Irish Republic flag from the GPO.

CHAPTER 9

DUBLIN CASTLE COURTYARD

Dublin Castle courtyard is very recognisable today from the many films that have used the wide scope of its courtyard and fine Georgian-style windows. It has also been much featured on TV news programmes, as a venue for the variety of tribunals before which suspect politicians are hauled from time to time.

From the very first Viking construction in Dublin, around AD 900, this area has been at the centre of the administration of the city. A mandate from King John in 1204 ordered the construction of a castle for his treasure, taxes and as a military base, a duty the Castle performed for over seven hundred years.

There is a statue of Justice above the old gate. Rather than wear a blindfold to indicate her lack of partiality, Justice here is almost smiling, with her eyes wide open. The scales that she holds are distinctive; if you look at them on a bright day you will see a small hole has been made in each of them. This is because rain used to collect in the scales unevenly, causing them to tip – Justice, therefore, becoming distinctly tilted. Furthermore, it is very noticeable that she faces away from the city and towards the Castle. Hence the ditty which summed up popular feeling toward British justice in 1916:

> *The statue of justice*
> *Mark well her station*
> *Her face to the Castle*
> *And her arse to the nation.*

AFTERMATH

As silence descended on a ruined city, the people of Dublin began to count up the cost. According to official estimates, 142 British soldiers and policemen had been killed. Sixty-four Volunteers had died, but the greatest casualties were amongst civilians, with an estimated 254 killed and some 2,000 wounded. Dublin's Fire Brigade chief estimated the cost of damaged buildings at £1.1 million, with stock lost amounting to about £0.75 million.

The stunned silence of the population soon gave way to outbursts of anger and recrimination – directed initially against the organisers and participants of the rebellion. Particularly vocal were the 'shawlies', whose income was dependent upon British pensions and income from relatives in the British Army. The rebellion threatened their livelihoods and they threw invective along with rotten vegetables and filth at the columns of prisoners being led through the city.

Yet looking ahead to the elections of December 1918, we find members of Sinn Féin sweeping the board. Many of the candidates for election, such as de Valera, Michael Collins and Countess Markievicz, had been participants in the Rising. Sinn Féin members won 73 of the 105 seats in Ireland. By contrast, John Redmond's respectable Irish Parliamentary Party won just six seats. Sinn Féin candidates stood on a platform of endorsement of the aims of the Rising. They made public their refusal to attend Westminster and their intention instead to assemble in Dublin, illegally if necessary, to create an Irish parliament, the first Dáil Éireann.

The writing on the wall had been there to see from the return of Sinn Féin prisoners in 1917, when massive crowds came out to cheer and greet them. Countess Markievicz took over two hours to travel through the crowds from her arrival in Westland Row Station to her home in Rathmines. Markievicz was the first woman ever elected to Westminster. Some sources mistakenly give Lady Astor as the name of the first woman elected to parliament; this is because, although elected, Markievicz refused to attend, joining Dáil Éireann instead as its first Minister for Labour. The story goes that, disguised, she did look in on Westminster, just to see had they allotted her the usual prerogatives – such as a coat peg with her name underneath.

EXECUTIONS

What explains the astonishing turnaround in the mood and outlook of the majority of the Irish population?

The first, and most immediate issue was that of the contrasting behaviour of the leaders of the two opposed sides in the days and weeks following the Rising. Whereas the rebel leaders were dignified, unshakeable and unashamed, General Maxwell, the *de facto* ruler of Ireland, was crude and brutal. Using sweeping powers of military rule, Maxwell arrested, court-martialled or detained 3,500 people – more than twice the number of participants in the Rising. His own thinking on the issue is recorded:

> In view of the gravity of the rebellion and its connection with German intrigue and propaganda, and in view of the great loss of life and destruction of property resulting therefrom, the General Officer Commanding-in-Chief, has found it imperative to inflict the most severe sentences on the known organisers of this detestable rising and on those Commanders who took an active part in the actual fighting which occurred. It is hoped that these examples will be sufficient to act as a deterrent to intriguers, and to bring home to them that the murder of His Majesty's liege subjects, or other acts calculated to imperil the safety of the Realm will not be tolerated.

Four days after the Rising, on 3 May, the first executions of its leaders took place: Pearse, MacDonagh and Clarke were shot at Kilmainham Gaol. The presence of a priest at the execution was refused.

Over the next nine days, the executions continued piecemeal. On 4 May, Edward Daly was executed, along with Willie Pearse,

Michael O'Hanrahan and Joseph Plunkett. Willie, younger brother of Pádraic and loyal follower, was not a senior figure amongst the rebels, but was fated by association. Joseph Plunkett requested permission to marry his fiancée, Grace Gifford. The ceremony took place at midnight; a few hours later, Plunkett was taken out to the yard and shot. The bodies were burned in quicklime rather than given to the relatives for burial.

The following day John MacBride was shot. Although playing a relatively minor role in the Rising, MacBride's marriage to the prominent Maud Gonne may well have tipped the scale as far as British intelligence was concerned. On 8 May, Colbert, Ceannt, Heuston and Mallin were executed.

Above left: Michael O'Hanrahan was a journalist, Gaelic League enthusiast and Second-in-Command in Jacobs' during the Rising. He was executed at dawn on 4 May 1916.

Above right: Thomas Kent was executed in Cork Detention Barracks on 9 May 1916. Kent's home was raided by the RIC (Royal Irish Constabulary) after the Rising in Dublin, as he and his brothers were known Republican activists. His brother was shot dead and Thomas Kent was arrested and hastily condemned to death.

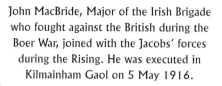

John MacBride, Major of the Irish Brigade who fought against the British during the Boer War, joined with the Jacobs' forces during the Rising. He was executed in Kilmainham Gaol on 5 May 1916.

By this time popular opinion was shifting markedly. The letters and final statements of the executed, along with the resolve with which they met their deaths, were introducing the leaders of the rebellion to a huge audience to whom they had previously been strangers.

The wiser Irish political figures, such as John Dillon, vehemently urged Prime Minister Asquith to bring 'Bloody' Maxwell under control and halt the executions. Asquith himself seems to have accepted the argument for leniency at this point and the government indicated that the executions had been halted. On 9 May, de Valera and Thomas Ashe had their sentences commuted. Was the cold elimination of the rebel leaders at an end? It seemed likely, with the Prime Minister intent on arriving in Dublin for 12 May.

However, Maxwell still had two prominent figures from the Rising in his hands – Mac Diarmada and Connolly. Both were signatories of the Proclamation, and if any two people could be singled out for having responsibility for the Rising, it was they: Mac Diarmada through his prominent and dynamic work for the IRB; Connolly for his leadership of the Irish Citizen Army. As far as Maxwell was concerned, they were the greatest traitors of all.

But it was not only Maxwell who desired to rid Ireland's political life of these men. William Martin Murphy, the leader of the employers in the bitter strike of 1913, was smarting at the damage done to his property as a result of the Rising. He was worried that, with Connolly left alive, the following for socialist ideas would soar. Murphy, a supporter of Home Rule for Ireland, used his newspaper, the *Irish Independent*, to campaign for Connolly's execution. One of a number of similar editorials (10 May) said:

> If these men are treated with too great leniency they will take it as an indication of weakness on the part of the government and the consequences may not be satisfactory. They may be more truculent than ever, and it is therefore necessary that society should be protected against their activity.

The dawn of 12 May, the day that Asquith arrived in Dublin, Connolly was taken from the Red Cross military hospital in Dublin Castle – where for five days British doctors and nurses had been trying to save his life – tied to a chair in the yard of Kilmainham Gaol, because his leg wound prevented him from standing, and shot. Mac Diarmada was executed the same morning.

An artist's impression of the execution of one of the rebels
in Kilmainham Gaol.

Soon after the executions, the literary and political work of the rebels became available and proved that far from being irresponsible criminals or German agents, the organisers of the Rising were motivated by high ideals. Continued deportations to internment camps were accompanied by revelations of British atrocity: the murder of civilians in North King Street and the attempted cover-up of the execution of Francis Sheehy Skeffington. Hanna, Sheehy Skeffington's widow, refused a clumsy apology and a large offer of compensation (£10,000), with admirable principle.

Along with these events, which shocked even the most moderate person in the country, general considerations also played their part behind the popular shift to radical nationalism. Britain's urgent need for troops for the war led her to try to introduce conscription on Irish males – a move met by outrage and an immensely popular general strike. Furthermore, the conservative nationalist strategy of John Redmond was increasingly wearing threadbare as British assurances to the leaders of Ulster Unionism made it clear they had no intention of giving Home Rule to all of Ireland.

Redmond himself was soon to regret his outspoken condemnation of the rebellion. He had quickly made clear his support for the British Administration on the day of the first execution, saying of the Rising:

> This attempted deadly blow at Home Rule is made more wicked and more insolent by the fact that Germany plotted it, Germany organised it and Germany paid for it.

It is hardly surprising, then, that the survivors of the Rising, together with a new generation of radicals, could rally the nation's desire for independence. General Maxwell himself had contributed indirectly to the re-emergence of militant nationalism, by interning so many prisoners in camps such as Frongoch in North Wales. It was there that the Volunteer officers who survived the Rising – notably Michael Collins – were able to pick up the pieces of the movement. The War of Independence, from 1919 to 1921, was conducted by the reorganised Volunteers, the Irish Republican Army, and was waged in the name of the elected representatives of Dáil Éireann. It was successful to the extent of winning self-government for the twenty-six counties of what is now the Republic of Ireland, precisely because of deep and heartfelt public support from the vast majority of the people.

There has been a trend in the history of the 1916 Rising to dismiss the effort of the rebels as irrational, bloodyminded and un-representative. But the pendulum of revisionism seems to be los-ing momentum. Now, in the new millennium, we can perhaps return to a more positive view of the events of Easter Week. Con-sidered from the point of view of the eventual enthusiastic and passionate support for the struggle for independence, the Rising cannot be faulted for its aims. The Rising may well have been a premature attempt to wrest the train of history from its rails, but ironically the subsequent experience of direct British military rule illustrated to hundreds of thousands the very points that patient

Countess Markievicz returns to a fine welcome from the citizens of Dublin on 21 June 1917, after her release from Aylesbury Prison.

nationalist argument had failed to establish.

A necessary sacrifice? Probably not. But the importance of the Rising should not be underplayed. It was a serious attempt at insurrection by people whose beliefs were soon to move from the fringe of political life to its very heart. Three future Taoisigh were participants in the Easter Rising: Seán Lemass, W.T. Cosgrave and, of course, Éamon de Valera.

> *All changed, changed utterly:*
> *A terrible beauty is born.*

W.B. Yeats, 'Easter 1916'

THE SIGNATORIES OF THE PROCLAMATION

Eamonn Ceannt (1881–1916)

Eamonn Ceannt, born in Ballymoe, Glenamaddy, County Galway, moved to Dublin with his family when he was ten years old. He took a £300 per annum position as a treasurer in Dublin Corporation, but his passion for Irish culture led him to become a teacher in the Gaelic League, and for several years he was a member of its *governing body (An* Coiste Gnótha). Keenly interested in traditional Irish music, he played the uilleann pipes, and during a pilgrimage to Rome in 1908 he played a selection of Irish airs for Pope Pius X.

A member of the IRB, he was one of the founding members of the Irish Volunteers in 1913 and became a member of their Provisional Committee. Two years later he was appointed, with Pearse and Clarke, to the Military Council, which planned the insurrection. Many of the first Council meetings were held in Ceannt's house in Dublin.

Ceannt was Commandant of the Fourth Battalion of the Irish Volunteers as well as being a member of the Provisional Government.

Thomas James Clarke (1857–1916)

Tom Clarke was born on the Isle of Wight to a Leitrim man (a British soldier) and a Tipperary woman, and his parents eventually settled in Dungannon, County Tyrone. Tom, already a member of the IRB, emigrated to America to find work in 1880, taking a position as an explosives operative for construction work on Staten Island. In America he formed close ties with John Devoy, leader of Clan na nGael. He was sent to London in 1883 by the IRB to put his new skills to work for their cause. He was captured with a case of liquid explosives and spent just over fifteen years in Chatham and Portland prisons. Upon his release, in 1898, he married Kathleen, a niece of one of his prison companions, John Daly, later Mayor of Limerick.

Clarke settled back in America but returned to Dublin in 1907, opening a small tobacconist's shop at 75a Parnell Street. This business premises was often used for meetings as he and his new friend, Seán Mac Diarmada, set about reviving the IRB and planning an uprising. His drooping moustache and quiet manner lent an air of diffidence to him, but it has been said that the largest file in Dublin Castle was marked Tom Clarke. As the oldest and most respected member of the Military Council, Clarke was given the honour of signing the Proclamation first.

James Connolly (1868–1916)

Born in Edinburgh, Scotland, to Irish emigrants living in desperate poverty, Connolly took a job as a printer's devil at the tender age of eleven and when he was fourteen joined the British Army. His seven years of service were spent in Cork where he educated himself, becoming more interested in socialism and nationalism. After getting married, Connolly returned to his native city where he befriended the Scottish socialist John Leslie, who converted him to Marx. He accepted a job in Dublin in 1896 as organiser for the Socialist Society. Within a few days of his arrival he founded the Irish Socialist Republican Party, and soon after established a newspaper, the *Workers' Republic*. The party proved a fairly unsuccessful venture, although Connolly was becoming renowned for his social thinking. He left for a trip to America, touring and lecturing until his return to Ireland, where he accepted the position of organiser for the Belfast branch of James Larkin's new union, the ITGWU (Irish Transport and General Workers' Union).

Connolly came to Dublin to help during the 1913 Lockout and was instrumental in founding the Irish Citizen Army. With the outbreak of war, Connolly began to agitate for a rising, and was brought into secret talks with the IRB. He was made Commander-General of the Rising.

Seán Mac Diarmada (1884–1916)

Seán Mac Diarmada was born in Corramore, Kiltyclogher, County Leitrim, and in his youth he worked in Glasgow, Scotland, as a gardener and then as a tram conductor. Later, in Belfast, he was sworn into the Irish Republican Brotherhood. In 1908 he was transferred to Dublin, where he developed a close personal and political friendship with Tom Clarke. From this time onwards he was unrelenting in his organisation of the IRB and through his travels across Ireland became the movement's best-known and most popular personality.

He was one of the founding members of the Irish Volunteers in 1913 and was secretary of the Supreme Council of the Irish Republican Brotherhood, member of the Military Council and member of the Provisional Government.

Thomas MacDonagh (1878–1916)

Born in Cloughjordan, County Tipperary, Thomas MacDonagh followed his parents into the teaching profession. His interest in the Irish language led him to join the Gaelic League, and it was while staying on the Aran Islands, off the coast of Galway, that he first encountered Pádraic Pearse. He joined the teaching staff of St Enda's and later, having taken a Masters Degree in Arts, he became a lecturer in English at University College, Dublin. With his friend Joseph Plunkett, he edited the *Irish Review* and was a director of the Irish Theatre. MacDonagh was often described as a wit, enthusiastic, a family man with never an unkind word to say about anyone. He was co-opted to the Military Council only weeks before the rebellion.

Pádraic Henry Pearse (1879–1916)

Pádraic Pearse's father was from England and his mother was from County Meath. Pádraic, born in Dublin, received his education from the Christian Brothers in Westland Row, and completed a degree in Arts and Law at the Royal University in 1901. Often described as an idealistic dreamer, he swore an oath with his younger brother, Willie, to free Ireland or die in the attempt. Physically he was tall, well built, with a slight stoop and deep eyes. Pearse abstained from the normal habits of young Irishmen, refusing to drink or smoke. There was one great love in his life, a student girl who tragically drowned. Through his poetry one can find the real Pearse:

> I tasted thy mouth, O sweetness of sweetness, and I hardened my heart, for fear of my staying.
>
> 'Renunciation'

His interest in the Irish language led Pearse to join the Gaelic League and he became the editor of its paper, *An Claidheamh Soluis*. Initially in his political career Pearse was a moderate, supporting the Home Rule movement, but he soon conceived the idea that independence would only be achieved by force and sacrifice. 'The old heart of the earth needed to be warmed with the red wine of the battlefield,' he wrote in 1915, about the Great War. Pearse was recruited to the IRB in 1912.

Pearse's school in Rathfarnham, St Enda's (*Scoil Éanna*), was a model for a new educational system, teaching his pupils through Gaeilge in an atmosphere of cultural learning and nationalism. The school is now a museum and a visit is recommended for those wishing to gain further insight into the first Provisional President of Ireland.

Joseph Mary Plunkett (1887–1916)

A poet and a scholar and the son of a papal count, Joseph had the benefit of close ties with the literary world. He was a friend of Thomas MacDonagh with whom he worked as director of the Irish Theatre and as co-editor of the *Irish Review*. Plunkett's house in Kimmage, a suburb to the south of Dublin, was used as one of the clearing stations for a cargo of arms landed at Howth in 1914 for the Irish Volunteers, and was also a training camp for young men who came from Britain for the Rising. Joseph Plunkett suffered from ill health and had had an operation for glandular tuberculosis only days before the rebellion, struggling out of his sickbed to partake in it. James Connolly said of him that he had the best military mind of all the signatories.

Joseph Plunkett was a member of the Military Council of the Provisional Government and of the Provisional Committee of the Irish Volunteers. He married his sweetheart, the artist Grace Gifford, in Kilmainham Gaol just hours before his execution.

Commemoration poster of the signatories of the Proclamation.

Bibliographical note

The Easter Rising is a relatively well-documented event, and there exists a large number of direct eyewitness accounts, generally from those Volunteers with a certain writing skill. Episodes of the Rising 'told by the men [sic] who made it' are to be found in collections such as *Dublin's fighting story 1916–1921,* or in newspaper articles over the years, especially those in the defence forces magazines, *An Cosantóir* or *An t-Óglách*. The newspapers of the day had their own accounts, with a certain amount of input from eyewitnesses, and the *Weekly Irish Times* issued a handbook on the rebellion with extensive lists of those arrested – now re-issued by Mourne River Press. *Dublin and the Sinn Féin Rising* (Hartnell) and *The Record of the Irish Rebellion of 1916* (Irish Life) were rival contemporary summaries.

While priests generally appeared to have been hostile to the rebels, in some instances making very public condemnation of the rebellion, the executed rebels were ministered to by a number of Capuchin fathers. The *Capuchin Annual* of 1942 is therefore an interesting read, with good photographs.

For an invaluable insight into the public mind, James Stephen's *The Insurrection in Dublin* is fascinating and highly readable.

All the above accounts and more, along with a certain amount of new oral testimony, are probably best brought together in a descriptive way in Max Caulfield's *The Easter Rebellion*, our recommendation for those wanting to read a longer account of the actual events of the Easter Rising.

Select Bibliography

Dublin and the Sinn Féin Rising, Hartnell & Co. (Dublin, 1916).

The Record of the Irish Rebellion of 1916, Irish Life (Dublin, 1916).

1916 Rebellion Handbook, first published *Weekly Irish Times, 1916,* reprint The Mourne River Press (Dublin, 1998).

The Irish Rebellion, postcard collection, Powel Press (Dublin 1916).

An Cosantóir, especially May 1966.

An t-Óglách, especially Vol IV (Dublin, 1926).

The Capuchin Annual, ed. Fr Henry OFM Cq. (Dublin, 1966).

Chronology Parts I–III, Ministry of Defence (Dublin 1949–50).

Dublin's fighting story 1916–21, told by the men who made it, The Kerryman Ltd., (Tralee, 1949).

Brennan-Whitmore, W.J., *Dublin Burning: the Easter Rising from Behind the Barricades*, Gill & Macmillan (Dublin, 1996).

Caulfield, Max, *The Easter Rebellion*, Gill & Macmillan (Dublin, 1995).

deCourcy Ireland, John, *The Sea and the Easter Rising*, Maritime Museum (Dún Laoghaire).

Griffith, Kenneth & O'Grady, Timothy E., *Curious Journey*, Hutchinson (London, 1982).

Hally, Col. P.J., *The Easter 1916 Rising in Dublin: The Military Aspects*, ' The Irish Sword', Vol. 7.

Heuston, John M., OP, *HQ Battalion, Easter Week 1916* (Dublin, 1966).

Hopkinson, Michael, ed., *Frank Henderson's Easter Rising*, Cork University Press (Cork, 1998).

Kostick, Conor, *Revolution in Ireland*, Pluto Press (London, 1996).

Lyons, F.S.L., *Ireland Since the Famine, Fontana (Glasgow, 1974).*

Mac Lochlain, Piaras F., *Last Words*, Kilmainham Gaol Restoration Society (Dublin, 1977).

McHugh, Roger, ed., *Dublin 1916*, Arlington Books (London, 1966).

O'Farrell, Padraic, *Who's Who in the Irish War of Independence and Civil War*, Lilliput Press (Dublin, 1997).

Ryan, Desmond, *The Easter Rising,* Golden Eagle Books (Dublin, 1949).

Spindler, Captain Karl, *The Mystery of the Casement Ship*, Anvil Books (Kerry, 1965).

Stephens, James, *The Insurrection in Dublin*, Mansel and Co. Ltd. (Dublin, 1916).

Other Walking Guides from
THE O'BRIEN PRESS

THE COMPLETE WICKLOW WAY
J.B. Malone

The Wicklow Way runs from Marley Park in south Dublin over the hills and glens of Wicklow, the 'garden of Ireland.' It brings you to such famous places as Glencree, Glenmalure, Glendalough, Powerscourt, Lough Dan, Annamoe and Laragh.
Paperback £5.99/$10.95/€7.61

KERRY WALKS
Kevin Corcoran

Covers the major scenic areas of Kerry, with twenty accessible walks around Kenmare, Dingle, Iveragh Peninsula and North Kerry. With a special section on Killarney – one of the most popular destinations in Ireland. Caters for all levels of walkers and all types of terrain.
Paperback £5.99/$10.95/€7.61

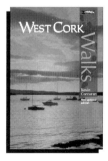

WEST CORK WALKS
Kevin Corcoran

Experience the rugged wildness of West Cork, often considered Ireland's most beautiful region. Ten different walks spread across West Cork, with clear instructions, maps, notable features along the way and beautiful wildlife illustrations by the author.
Paperback £5.99/$10.95/€7.61

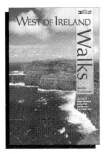

WEST OF IRELAND WALKS
Kevin Corcoran

Spectacular walking routes in the counties of Clare, Galway and Mayo. There is a huge choice of landscape to the walker – mountain peaks, woodland, bogs and lakes, sandy beaches and the strange limestone plateaux of the Burren.

Paperback £5.99/$10.95/€7.61

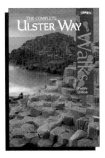

THE COMPLETE ULSTER WAY
Paddy Dillon

This is the only walking guide to incorporate the entire Ulster Way: an 1,070km stretch across all the most beautiful parts of Northern Ireland's six counties, from mountain landscape at the Mournes to seascapes at the Giant's Causeway and the Antrim coastline, as well as lakeland and pastoral lands. Includes forty-one walks in all, with detailed instructions and maps.   Paperback £9.99/$15.95/€12.68

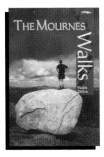

THE MOURNES WALKS
Paddy Dillon

Thirty-two walks covering all parts of the Mourne Mountains, including the High and Low Mournes as well as the Kingdom of Mourne; the Silent Valley circuit; the Mourne Coastal Path; the old smuggling route of the Brandy Pad; Warrenpoint and Rostrevor and the complete Mourne Wall route. Detailed instructions are provided, along with location maps outlining each walk.

Paperback £5.99/$10.95/€7.61

Also from The O'Brien Press

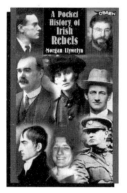